D0895105

cop.1

q   Anderson, Erica
B   The Schweitzer album.
Schweitzer

THE SCHWEITZER
ALBUM

THE
SCHWEITZER
ALBUM

A Portrait in Words and Pictures by

ERICA ANDERSON

Additional text by Albert Schweitzer

NEW YORK: HARPER & ROW, PUBLISHERS
LONDON: ADAM AND CHARLES BLACK

First Edition

Library of Congress Catalog Card Number 65–20444

Printed by Conzett & Huber in Zürich, Switzerland
Produced in association with Chanticleer Press, Inc., New York

First British Edition 1965 by A. & C. Black Ltd., London

To Albert Schweitzer
in gratitude for his lifetime
of dedication to humanity

ACKNOWLEDGMENTS

I first met Dr. Schweitzer in March 1950, when I went to Lambarene hoping to obtain his permission to make a motion picture of his life and work. The film *Albert Schweitzer* was first shown in Boston in 1957. Since 1950 I have made nineteen trips to Lambarene. My collection of photographs, including approximately seven thousand in color and twenty-six thousand in black and white, was made during these visits and during Dr. Schweitzer's European sojourns in 1952, 1953, 1955, 1957, and 1959, the year of his last trip to Europe. I am deeply grateful to him for his kindness in resigning himself to the constant pursuit of my cameras.

I should like to express my gratitude to Mme. Emmy Martin of Günsbach, who has made available to me photographs of Dr. Schweitzer's early life, and to all the members of the hospital staff at Lambarene and of the Günsbach household who have endured me and my cameras for the past fifteen years.

I am grateful also to Felix and Richard Meiner of Hamburg for permission to use the draft of Dr. Schweitzer's letter to Felix Meiner; to Dr. Howard C. Rice and the Princeton University Library, where an Albert Schweitzer collection has been begun, for permission to use the photographs of the Schweitzer pamphlet on Eugene Münch, the thesis title page for *The Psychiatric Study of Jesus,* and the Congo Mission article; and to Miss Laura Persons, who is compiling a Schweitzer bibliography and verified for me the original source of various documents.

Jeannette Hopkins' help in the preparation of this book has been a joy and inspiration to me. Her untiring and enthusiastic work has been truly vital, and I am fully aware that without her I would have faltered. Her selectivity of judgment, her clarity of mind, and her sensitivity of heart transformed chaos into coherence. I am deeply grateful.

BIBLIOGRAPHICAL NOTE

The letters, documents, and memorabilia quoted or reproduced in this book have been given to me by Dr. Schweitzer over the years. The quotations from his conversation or speeches and writings have been translated from the French or German for this book. A number of these quotations are from my notebooks. The "Paris Notes" were written by Dr. Schweitzer in 1959 in preparation for a speech; the "Brussels Notes" were set down in the same year for a similar occasion. The comments at Copenhagen were from a 1959 interview with an American journalist on the occasion of Dr. Schweitzer's trip to Denmark to receive the Sonning Prize for service to humanity. I had been asked to translate his remarks into English and recorded them at the time. The 1953 Brazzaville interview was obtained by a member of the staff of Radio Brazzaville, and these excerpts of the tape were translated from the French. The 1963 Lambarene interview with Dr. Schweitzer was conducted by a group of journalists from Radio Gabon, Libreville, on April 18, on the occasion of his fiftieth anniversary at Lambarene; the excerpts used were translated from a copy of the original tape. The speech of that same date was made at the Air France hotel in Lambarene to a group of old friends. It, too, was transcribed from a tape, given to me by Dr. Berthold Weisberg, formerly government hospital physician in Lambarene. Dr. Schweitzer's comments at Hamburg were taped and transcribed for me by the schools at which he spoke. His words on his boyhood in Günsbach in Part I have been translated from original material which he prepared for the German version of the movie *Albert Schweitzer*, but which was not used in the final script.

The reproduction of the portrait of Dr. Schweitzer by Augustus John appeared in the London *Sunday Times* of October 23, 1955.

CONTENTS

THE SCHWEITZER
ALBUM

"How wonderful it is that in my old age I can be at home where I was in my youth, that the themes of the beginning of the symphony of my life resound in the finale." A. S.

I
THE THEMES
OF
THE BEGINNING

It is not inappropriate for Schweitzer's life to be thought of in terms of music, a symphony of themes that taken together form a pattern of power and beauty. The themes of his life are many—devotion to truth and reason, a quality of independence, loyalty to ideals and to friends, a sensitivity to the suffering of others and a reverence for all life, a high sense of duty and responsibility, idealism tempered with practicality, a single-minded dedication to chosen ends, a commitment in religious discipleship to follow in the way of Jesus the Nazarene.

In Schweitzer many of the talents of his forebears are united. His paternal grandfather was a schoolmaster and organist; so were three of his great-uncles. His mother was the daughter of a Munster Valley pastor who loved organs and was skilled in organ-building. His father was the pastor of an evangelical Protestant congregation.

Soon after Albert Schweitzer's birth on January 14, 1875, at Kaysersberg in Upper Alsace in the shadow of a medieval castle, the family moved to Günsbach fifteen miles away, and it is in Günsbach that his European home has been ever since. He has returned there on rare visits whenever his work in Africa permitted.

The small boy began piano lessons at five and composed harmonies for hymns at seven; at eight he started to play the organ. Under Eugene Münch a passion for Bach was awakened in him; and at twenty-three he wrote his first published work, a twenty-eight-page leaflet in tribute to Münch at his death. From Charles Marie Widor of Paris, he learned perfection of technique, the precision of the dedicated artist. In his autobiography he acknowledges his gratitude to these masters. He learned a sense of duty from one schoolmaster and a love of philosophy and history from another. At Strasbourg University, where he enrolled in 1893 in the theological college, he began a study of religious philosophy that has continued throughout his life. With a rigorous clarity of mind that emerged early, when as a child of eight he first questioned contradictions in the Bible, he studied the scholarly findings of his elders with penetrating intelligence and decided, at times, that they were wrong. This habit of freedom of thought was encouraged in childhood by his mother and father and by his professors; his eager and curious mind unfolded in the warmth of their understanding.

But even as his thought disturbed the traditional positions of Biblical scholarship, he held firmly to his view that truth, however new and unexpected, cannot damage religious faith. His quest for the historical Jesus led to a Jesus that differed from the person described by earlier scholars. It led, also, to a commitment of discipleship no less strong for the rigor of his quest. Truth pursued in freedom ended in love. There is no foundation stronger than this.

Ever since boyhood Schweitzer had believed that his happiness and good fortune in a world full of pain was a gift that ought to be repaid. As a child he had prayed for all living things and tried to protect life where he could; the suffering of others was his own. In obedience to his sense of commitment, he decided to work until he was thirty years old in the fields of scholarship and music and then to devote himself, for the rest of his life, to the service of men. He tried first to help abandoned and neglected children, then homeless men and tramps, but failed in both efforts to find a place for himself among the organized institutions of community welfare. His wish was to help in a personal way, as an individual acting in freedom. One autumn morning in 1904 he came upon a magazine article, "Henry Chapuis et les Besoins de la Mission du Congo," on the needs of the Congo mission. It ended with the words: "Des hommes qui sachent, sur un geste du Roi, dire: 'Maitre, je pars,' voila ce dont l'Eglise a besoin." ("Men who can say, at a sign from the King, 'Master, I go forth,' that is what the Church needs.") Schweitzer's life was to be his response.

Nine years later he was ready, ignoring the reproaches of relatives and friends who voiced fears that his talents would be buried among savages, ignoring the warnings of the Paris Missionary Society that his lack of theological orthodoxy might cause them to oppose his acceptance. Schweitzer added to his degrees in philosophy and theology a third in medicine, preaching and lecturing throughout the exhausting years of his medical study. Some of his most noted books were published during this time. Then, with his bride Helene Bresslau, who alone among his friends encouraged him and who had trained as a nurse to be able to help him, he bought medicines and hospital equipment, and offered his services to the Paris Missionary Society. Its members requested a meeting to examine into his theological beliefs; he avoided the confrontation and offered instead to talk privately with each member. Not theological orthodoxy but commitment to serve ought to be the test, he maintained. He promised to practice medicine and not to

These photographs of Schweitzer's mother, Adele Schillinger Schweitzer, and father, Louis Schweitzer, hang on the wall of his Günsbach bedroom.

preach, a promise from which, to his great joy, he was later to be released. On Good Friday in 1913 he left Günsbach for Lambarene.

The themes of the beginning were to recur throughout his life. Prepared to sacrifice the music he loved, he found he was able to continue his organ practice even in the jungle. Prepared to sacrifice the teaching and preaching which had brought him deep happiness, he was to lecture at many universities in the decades to come, and to preach each Sunday to the hospital community. Prepared to sacrifice his influence as philosopher and scholar and to accept oblivion and isolation in the jungle, he found years later that his influence had spanned the world. The example of his life of service had touched the hearts of strangers as the theory alone could never have done.

Schweitzer's mother was a shy, proud woman, well informed and well read. His father was a strong, kind man, of high ideals and intellect, who encouraged his son to explore freely within the realm of ideas. Schweitzer has described his father as his "dearest friend." When the boy was born, his father was so delighted that he leapt for joy over the cradle, frightening his wife. Both parents stimulated in the boy a love of learning and a devotion to ethics.

"In the spring of 1913, I went to Günsbach to say good-by to my parents. It was the last time I would see my mother, who was to be run down and killed by military troops during the war. It was not in either of our natures to express in words the love we felt for one another. But we understood each other without speaking." Schweitzer's mother was killed in 1916; his father died at 80 in 1925.

Albert Schweitzer as a boy, about five years old, the earliest picture known.

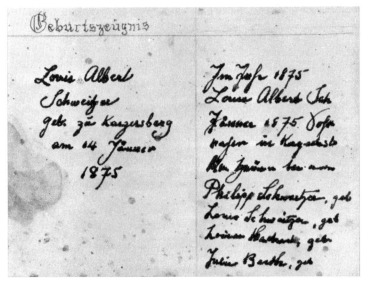

The birth certificate for Albert Schweitzer, born in Kaysersberg, Alsace, on January 14, 1875, the second child and first son of Louis Schweitzer and Adele Schillinger Schweitzer.

"It was to me a special mystery how the raindrop, the snowflake, and the hailstone were formed, and I was hurt that people did not recognize the absolute mystery of nature, but rather spoke confidently about what made them, succeeding only in producing descriptions which made the mysterious more mysterious. Already when I was a child it was clear to me that what we call the force of life remains, according to its own being, inexplicable. Even today when I see the light broken into many colors in a water pitcher, I am capable of forgetting everything around me and cannot tear myself away from that image." A. S.

Albert Schweitzer with his classmates, about seven years old.

"I long once more to have the freedom to live in memories, to be allowed to wander among them. I recognize how wonderful it is that in my old age I can be at home where I was in my youth, that the themes of the beginning of the symphony of my life resound again in the finale.

"This privilege is to be twice valued in a time when so many men, as a result of the terrible events of two wars, are denied the right to enjoy the home of their youth. This loss has brought homesickness to their hearts.

"Yet to me it has been given in my old age to be at home in the village in which I grew up, in the surroundings where I received my first impressions. Because of the demands of the work of my student days I had to deny myself much that I longed for. But I do not want to give up now the heartfelt wish which I have cherished so long of enjoying the splendor of being at home once more and searching out those places that remind me of my youth. So let me, after these long years of work, be lighthearted again in the most beautiful sense of that word. The autumn sun calls to me; there is no autumn sun in Africa, only here.

"I remember four or five periods of my life when nature spoke to me here when I was small, before I went to school. In the vineyards which my father had newly planted and which bore their first harvest, my father called me to hunt for grapes. When I found none, he showed me finally where some were hidden in the leaves. And here along the line of the brook, in the small valley behind the hills, we walked to the interior of the Günsbach valleys. Here at these rocks I used to sit so often during my later student days, reflecting on my plan to go to Africa to help. Here in the meadow covered with flowers we rested. And then we went further up on a winding mountain trail. And suddenly the valley stopped, shut off from the world outside. Here the mountains drew together and I could no longer see the way to the valley leading to the plain.

"I came here many times before leaving for Africa, to experience the mystery of remoteness from the world. Here on the path along the

Albert Schweitzer's birthplace at Kaysersberg, Alsace—the parsonage with the small turret. A few weeks after his birth the family moved fifteen miles away to Günsbach, where his European home has been ever since.

woods one can look beyond the valley onto the plain and the world. My mother loved this path and this view. Always in the first days of vacation we came here with her and rested in the grass. I would suggest that the ruins at the end of the valley lifting high above the plain be the boundary for our excursion. Lying on the wall, I looked down on the castle and considered what would rule my life. How I have loved the castles of Alsace! In the shadow of the proud castle of Kaysersberg, I was born. Often I have returned to it, to the wonderful church at the foot of the hilltop castle. I always imagine that men such as I who are rooted in the past have a special relationship to it for their entire lives.

"Now I come down into the valley to a small mountain lake. How often we walked here with my mother after the four-hour journey from Günsbach, to sit here with her. When she came down from the high mountains around the end of the valley she would say, 'Here, children, I am completely at home. Here among the rocks, among the woods. I came here as a child. Let me breathe the fragrance of the fir trees and enjoy the quiet of this refuge from the world. Do not speak. After I am no longer on the earth, come here and think of me.' I do think of you, Mother. I love as you did this refuge from the world, this niche.

"Now I have left the mountains and the castles and the woods. I stand before the church and see the swallows once more. The swallows are gathering for the journey south. We will set out together. But a time will come when I will not see you when you gather for this journey, and you will set out for the south without me, for I will have gone on a longer journey from one world to another. Hurry with your going, so that cold and death from starvation do not surprise you here! Farewell, until we meet in Africa under the southern sky." A. S.

A family portrait, around 1882. Adele, Albert, Margrit, and Louise. Paul, Schweitzer's brother, had not yet been born. A sixth baby, a girl, died in infancy.

Albert Schweitzer's first "autograph," written to a friend of his sister in Güns-bach when he was about six years old.

Family photograph with Louise, Albert, Adele (standing), Margrit, Paul, and their parents.

Albert Schweitzer, about seventeen years of age, with his brother and sisters in family snapshots taken in the garden and at the parsonage at Günsbach, apparently on the same day. Top, left to right, Adele, Pauli, Louise, Albert, unidentified girl, Margrit; below, left to right, Albert, Pauli, Margrit, unidentified girl, Adele, Louise.

Schweitzer as a young man, about twenty-one years of age.

EUGÈNE MUNCH

1857–1898

Selig sind die Toten, die in dem Herrn
sterben, von nun an; Ja der Geist spricht,
dass sie ruhen von ihrer Arbeit; denn
ihre Werke folgen ihnen nach.

Offenb. Johannes, Kap. 14 Vers 13.

1898
IMPRIMERIE J. BRINKMANN, MULHOUSE.

The title page of Albert Schweitzer's first published writing, Eugene
Münch, 1857–1898, *a memorial brochure privately printed in 1898.
Schweitzer had studied with Münch, then organist at the Reformed
Church of St. Stephen in Mülhouse. When Münch died, Schweitzer
contributed to this memorial booklet. He was twenty-three years old.*

In 1902 Schweitzer gave his first lecture before the Theological Faculty at Strasbourg. During the same period he was principal of the Theological College (Collegium Wilhelmitanum), keeping as his study the room he had occupied as a student. Here, with his students of the college.

Schweitzer's calling card, used during his academic career, noting his licentiate of theology and his doctorate of philosophy.

Albert Schweitzer
Lic. theol.   Dr. phil.
Privatdozent a. d. K. W. Universität

Thomasstaden. 1ª

This melancholy African Negro, part of a monument to General Bruat by Bartholdi, sculptor of the Statue of Liberty, stood in the town square at Colmar and deeply impressed Albert Schweitzer as a small boy. Whenever he went with his family to Colmar, he asked if they would detour to the Champ de Mars to see it, and during his student years he often visited the site, meditating on the cruelty of the white man to the black. Years later he went to Africa to serve the Negro as a penance for the years of oppression other white men had imposed. A plaster copy of the Negro head stands today on the table in his Günsbach bedroom.

"His face with its sad, thoughtful expression spoke to me of the misery of the Dark Continent." A. S.

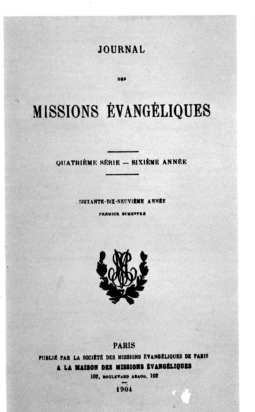

JOURNAL

DES

MISSIONS ÉVANGÉLIQUES

QUATRIÈME SÉRIE — SIXIÈME ANNÉE

SOIXANTE-DIX-NEUVIÈME ANNÉE

PREMIER SEMESTRE

PARIS

PUBLIÉ PAR LA SOCIÉTÉ DES MISSIONS ÉVANGÉLIQUES DE PARIS
A LA MAISON DES MISSIONS ÉVANGÉLIQUES
102, BOULEVARD ARAGO, 102

1904

SOCIÉTÉ DES MISSIONS ÉVANGÉLIQUES DE PARIS 389

HENRY CHAPUIS
et les besoins de la Mission du Congo.

Dieu vient de rappeler à Lui un modeste et fidèle serviteur de notre œuvre. Henry Chapuis, artisan-missionnaire au Congo, nous a été repris le 6 mai dernier, à Genève.

Il était né le 20 avril 1876 et avait appris le métier de serrurier. Placé de bonne heure sous l'influence et dans l'atmosphère vivifiante de l'œuvre de l'Étoile, membre de l'Église libre, ami d'Ivan Mercier, il s'était offert d'abord en 1897, puis en février 1901, pour l'œuvre des Missions. Cette même année, en octobre, il fut accepté; dans les mois qui suivirent il compléta sa préparation par divers apprentissages. Sa destination fut incertaine pendant quelque temps. Il avait lui-même pensé au Zambèze, et, pendant quelque temps à Madagascar; en dernier lieu ce fut au Congo que ses services furent attribués. Il s'embarqua le 15 décembre 1901, à Bordeaux et depuis lors il rendit à la mission les plus fidèles et les plus dévoués services.

Dans toutes les stations où il fut employé, son travail et son caractère furent hautement appréciés par nos missionnaires. En dernier lieu, son activité fut consacrée à la station de Talagouga. C'est là qu'il ressentit les atteintes de la fièvre et que, dès les premiers mois de cette année, la nécessité d'un rapatriement s'imposa à lui.

Sa femme qui, au début, avait été retenue à Genève par un enfant nouveau-né, l'avait rejoint au bout de quelques mois. Elle ne put partager sa vie de missionnaire que pendant un temps assez court; dans le commencement de 1903, elle avait dû rentrer en Europe, un an avant son mari.

consécration. »

M. Coillard racontait un jour son émotion en voya[nt] les plus grands chefs d'un roi africain, sur un geste d[e] sa part, se lever et se mettre en route avec cette simp[le] parole : « Maître, je pars ».

Des hommes qui sachent, sur un geste du Roi, dire « Maître, je pars », voilà ce dont l'Église a besoin.

The article in the Paris Journal des Missions Evangelique *that stirred Schweitzer with its call to serve in the Congo Mission. He decided to become a physician and nine years later applied to the Mission for an African post.*

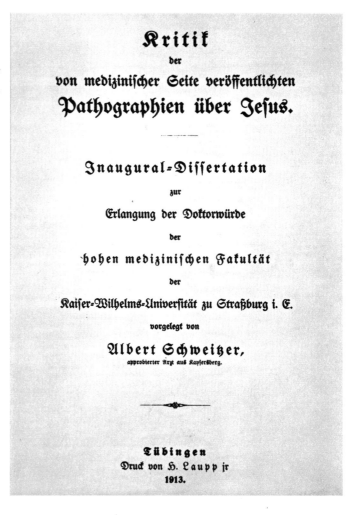

The title page of Schweitzer's thesis for the doctorate of medicine, presented at the University of Strasbourg in 1913 and published that same year: The Psychiatric Study of Jesus. The first edition in English appeared in 1948. It added to his earlier Quest of the Historical Jesus (1906) valuable scholarly insights into the nature and importance of Jesus. Schweitzer arranged organ concerts to help pay for the printing of this thesis.

Kritik
der
von medizinischer Seite veröffentlichten
Pathographien über Jesus.

Inaugural-Dissertation

zur

Erlangung der Doktorwürde

der

hohen medizinischen Fakultät

der

Kaiser-Wilhelms-Universität zu Straßburg i. E.

vorgelegt von

Albert Schweitzer,
approbierter Arzt aus Kaysersberg.

Tübingen
Druck von H. Laupp jr
1913.

After his medical studies, Schweitzer wrote to Monsieur *Boegner, and a fragment of the draft from which the original was copied is reproduced here, with the full text of the letter offering his services in the Gabon. He went to Africa in 1913.*

The first mission station at Lambarene at which the Schweitzers served overlooked the river, the forest, and the hills. It had been built in 1876 by American missionaries, and when the Gabon became a French colony it became attached to the Societe des Missions de Paris.

Strasbourg

M. Boegner, Director
Societe des Missions Evangeliques
Boulevard Arayo 102
Paris

Dear M. Boegner:

It's been a long time since I have sent you any word of myself. Forgive me. I had to work very hard to prepare for my medical examinations. Now they are behind me. Everything went very well. And now we can discuss our projects. First, let me ask if you and the committee of the Society of Missions have definitely decided to accept me as a doctor for one of your missions in Gabon. Let me be clear: I am not suggesting that I come as someone who will be an expense for you. My hospital is not to be supported by you. I want to find the means to found it and provide for its running expenses myself. I am counting on devoted friends who have given me to understand that they will help me within the limits of their capacities. So, my hospital will cost your Society nothing. I would feel very badly to think of asking you for anything at all. For I know what heavy expenses the overseas missions represent for you. Will you please first tell me whether you agree to my proposal to come on the conditions I have outlined.

With warm thoughts of you, I am,

Yours devotedly,
Albert Schweitzer

Almost 2,000 patients were treated in the first nine months at Schweitzer's first hospital. The first building turned over to Schweitzer in 1913 by the Protestant mission still stands. It was home, pharmacy, and office. Patients were treated in the open air until an old hen house was converted into a small treatment center. By the end of one year, several new buildings had been erected.

During World War I the Schweitzers, as Alsatians, were forbidden to practice medicine and, in 1917, were interned as prisoners of war in France; first in a Bordeaux barracks, then in the internment camp at Garaison in the Pyrenees, shown here; then at St. Remy de Provence. Schweitzer wears the wooden shoes of a prisoner. During this forced separation from his hospital, he worked on his book Philosophy of Civilization.

After three years of internment, Schweitzer returned to Strasbourg, ill and unhappy to be kept from his chosen work. But lectures and concerts, study and writing, brought him new strength. In 1924 he returned to Africa.

On Schweitzer's return to Africa, he found the hospital buildings decayed. Soon he had repaired them, only to face the crisis of an epidemic and a shortage of space for the patients who flocked to seek his help. He decided to build a new hospital on a larger site three miles upstream. In 1927 the hospital moved to its present location.

An early picture, dated around 1927, showing volunteers packing supplies for the Lambarene hospital. Neighbors in Günsbach and Strasbourg make packing cases for the supplies. Other volunteers help the Lambarene hospital by sewing mosquito netting, rolling bandages, stitching operating gowns. Headquarters is a house in the Rue des Greniers in Strasbourg, where the cases are prepared for shipment to Bordeaux. Many of the original volunteers—and their sons and daughters—still work there today.

Contents of crates destined for shipment to Africa detailed in Schweitzer's handwriting.

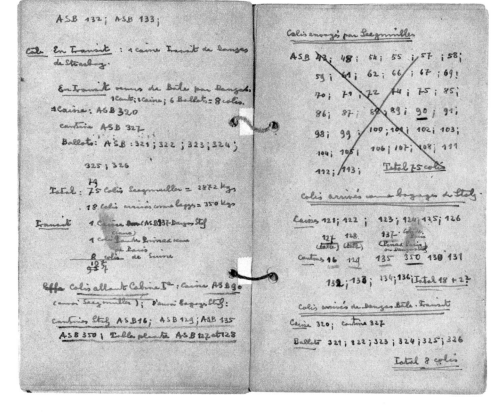

Over the years, on his return trips to Europe, Schweitzer gave organ concerts—because he loved to play and in order to raise necessary funds for the hospital.

A fragment of Schweitzer's music notations.

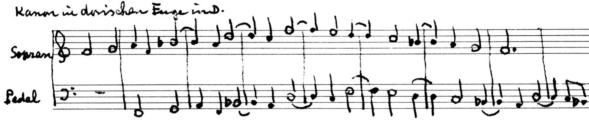

Schweitzer respects the careful craftsmanship of earlier days, particularly of organs, as this telegram to a correspondent in Oregon shows. He has done much to save old organs from being replaced by newer ones.

Dear Reverend Weinland:

It has taken me a long time to answer the very kind letter which you sent to Mr. Fritz Dickert and myself. I could not do it from Africa and when I returned in September 1959 to Europe I had to start traveling for a number of weeks. I have now come back from these trips, which took me through Germany, Switzerland, Denmark, Sweden, Belgium and Holland, and Paris, also. Now I can start with my correspondence—the letter to you is one of the first from my pen.

I am deeply moved that the American Guild of Organists of your chapter wants to help to keep intact the organ which I planned and rebuilt—an organ I consider the model of a good village organ. This organ was built after the first one, built at the end of the seventeenth century, was destroyed in the first war. Not until 1932 did we have the means to build the present organ. But we could not construct it the way we wanted to: at that time the organ builders had not relearned the use of the old *sommiers* and mechanical tracker action, and we had to use modern *sommiers* and tubular pneumatic instead.* Also, to save money we had to re-use as many as possible of the wood and metal pipes from the old organ, but they were no longer suitable and served us only for a limited time. We now have to substitute, for the old bad material, good material which will serve for a long time to come. The cost of material for these substitutions will unfortunately be quite substantial. But there is no point in restoring the organ without thinking ahead so that it can be done in the best way possible.

It is a great asset that Mr. Alfred Kern, to whom we have entrusted the work, knows the ways of the great organ builders: Cavaille-Coll, builder of the organs of Saint Sulpice and Notre Dame in Paris, and an artist in tuning, was the teacher of the founder of the firm Haerpfer, who built our organ in 1932. In 1880 Haerpfer settled as organ builder in Boulay, West Alsace, where he created a series of beautifully tuned organs. His son Frederick Haerpfer had inherited his knowledge of the art of tuning an organ, and proved it when he built the big organ for the concert room at Strasbourg. From him two men learned the art and secret of tuning as Cavaille-Coll had known it. One of them was Mr. Alfred Kern. I have known him for years and have followed and helped him as he developed into a master organ tuner. He guarantees that the organ will retain its beautiful sound in spite of the rebuilding, that it will still be an organ on which one can play the pre-Bach masters and also J. S. Bach, Mendelssohn, Cesar Franck, Widor, Guilmant, Reger. It will be in reality the model of a village organ.

For this reason we dare, the organist and I, to ask you to help us find the means necessary for rebuilding. The communities of Günsbach and Griesbach, which are supposed to pay for it, suffered greatly during the two wars. In each war the church tower was destroyed and had to be rebuilt. Furthermore, the woods from which Günsbach gets some income were much damaged by gunfire, and the income is much less than it used to be. Günsbach also needs a new water system, and altogether can contribute only very little for the organ which we need so much. The promise that the organ will survive means a great deal to me.

Of all the organs I helped to build, the most beautiful of them perished during the wars. The type of organ I built in Günsbach in 1932 I considered ideal for a village—I had concentrated for many years on this problem. If through this the organ is saved, this will permit me a happiness in my old age. For this reason I dare, with the organist, to approach people far from here. It will cost about $15,000 (fifteen thousand dollars) to put it in good condition as an example of the ideal village organ. . . .

I thank you in advance for all you are ready to do.

With our best greetings,
Albert Schweitzer and Fritz Dickert

* A method of organ building antedating electropneumatic organs and still in considerable favor.

33

On June 18, 1912, Schweitzer married Helene Bresslau, daughter of the director of historical studies at Strasbourg University. He had known her when she was a student, and it was with Helene that he planned to begin his mission in Africa.

Schweitzer with his daughter Rhena, who was born on his own birthday, January 14, in 1919.

Schweitzer on the hillside near the Ogowe River at his jungle hospital during the first years.

Mme. Emmy Martin has been Schweitzer's European representative since 1927. She had great talent as a singer, but after the death of her husband, a minister and friend of Schweitzer, she put aside a promising career to devote her life to the hospital. Now in her eighties, she still continues to serve the hospital, living in Günsbach.

"A Christian is one who has the spirit of Christ. This is the only theology." A. S.

II
THE FELLOWSHIP
OF
THE SPIRIT

To Schweitzer all life is one: every creature depends on others, and all are entitled to respect and care. *Thou shalt not kill* is the commandment to men, bidding them sacrifice no living plant or animal needlessly, and even under compulsion of absolute necessity, when duty compels such sacrifice, to respond with sorrow.

He carries his philosophy into the life of his hospital, where animals are accorded a place of safety and live in peace with each other. A bee that has invaded the dining room will be caught gently—not killed—and released outside. When a column of ants invaded a visitor's room, he asked her to move into another until they had crossed through and gone their way. "Don't be cruel to them," he said. He urges workers to watch as they dig to avoid harming insects, nor will he permit the wood of building posts to be treated with chemicals that could endanger insect life. Instead he counts on the toughness of the timber to be its own protection. "I use wood that is termite-proof. If they still dare to nibble on it, they will have to go to a dentist afterward!"

No bird or animal in the hospital village—hen or pig or sheep—is killed for food. Fish and crocodile meat brought by fishermen are occasionally served at table, but Schweitzer himself in recent years has given up eating either meat or fish, even the liver dumplings he used to relish and enjoy. "I can't eat anything that was alive any more." When a man questioned him on his philosophy and said that God made fish and fowl for people to eat, he answered, "Not at all.

Only when a creature can't exist without feeding on other animals may it be fed so. When natives bring pelicans whose wings are clipped and they can't fish for themselves, I feed them fish, but always with a feeling of sadness and guilt." To visitors who asked what to do with a young antelope they had purchased from a hunter who had killed its mother, he said, "Unsweetened milk, air, sun, shade, and love for the antelope—but what did you do to the hunter?"

Plants, too, are under his protection, and even the sight of cut flowers brings him pain. He asked a staff member one day to tell a visitor who picked a bouquet for a nurse's birthday to do so no more. "Tell him if you can, in a subtle way, that flowers are not to be broken. Reverence for life is practiced here." He will change the location of a new building to save one tree.

All living creatures are included in his philosophy, all races and conditions of men— black and white, rich and poor, healthy and sick. An injured patient arrived in a boat one day. "Refuse him, Doctor," urged a hospital attendant. "He was here before and stole the very drugs he was healed with and sold them in the village. A thief he is and has no claim on us again."

"What would the Lord Jesus have answered when someone came to Him in pain?" Schweitzer asked. "Quick, waste no time. Get him to the operating room."

" 'Whatsoever you do unto the least of these my brethren, you have done it unto me.' This is my image of the Kingdom of God—not the Apocalypse—only *this* is the right meaning."

Schweitzer reproaches himself for every act on his part of seeming failure to respect the needs of life. He tells, for example, how shortly after the end of World War II he performed a concert of chamber music in Barcelona. When the oboe players performed clumsily, his companions made fun of them and he did not object. But later he discovered that the men were really great artists. They had played badly because, after years of starvation, they had just finished their first good meal, and in their eagerness had eaten too much to be able to control their breathing properly. Schweitzer has never forgiven himself for judging them harshly.

It is because of this profound respect for all life that he has fought against the development, testing, and use of nuclear arms. "What would Jesus have answered if questioned about the atomic bomb?" he asked a group of ministers. " 'O, Ihr Klein gläubigen!' " ("Oh, ye of little faith!") He urged them to speak out against nuclear warfare, and deplored the reluctance of the churches to take such a lead. "Atom-waffen sind nicht nur eine Sünde; sie sind auch eine Schande." ("Atomic weapons are not only a sin; they are also a desecration.")

The idea of reverence for life will spread from one person to another, he believes, not by mass meetings or radio or television: "One must speak to the heart of the individual; only then does one feel the power of the idea."

(In response to a discouraged friend) "Never say there is nothing beautiful in the world any more. There is always something to make you wonder in the shape of a leaf, the trembling of a tree." A. S.

"How can ethics become the basis for a world philosophy? When it relates to the entire world; when it forms and builds our spiritual relationship to the world. It does that only if it shows us how we are linked with all living things. As the wave in the ocean surges forward together with all waves, so must we feel in our life the life that is around us, with its privations and its anguish. Then we will have an ethical code that is meaningful and can sustain a world philosophy. I have ventured to express the thought that the basic concept on which goodness rests is reverence for all life—the great mystery in which we find ourselves together with all living things." A. S.

Parsifal, Schweitzer's pelican who used to follow him about, was free to wander as he would, swimming on the Ogowe River, flying in the jungle. He returned every night.

Animals wait for scraps and peacefully share the same dish. The goats enjoy using the cellar door as a slide.

On the steps leading to Schweitzer's room, a goat and a chicken take their ease as they often do. One chicken insisted on spending the night in his room and, let out in the morning, went about her business and returned again each evening. When she turned up with a friend, Schweitzer decided the custom was at an end.

25.4.53

Mr. Schweitzer:
Something very nice happened. A poor old man who has been here in the Nouvelle Case [a new building] for a long time received rice as his ration. He chased away a chicken that wanted to partake of his rice. I told him to be good to the chicken and to let it eat of his rice; which, after some hesitation, he did. Then the chicken sat down in the rags of his bed and out of gratitude it laid a beautiful egg. His joy was great.

Ali
[A Dutch nurse]

"In the past we have tried to make a distinction between animals which we acknowledge have some value and others which, having none, can be liquidated when and as we wish. This standard must be abandoned. Everything that lives has value simply as a living thing, as one manifestation of the mystery that is life. And let us not forget that some of the more evolved animals show that they have feelings and are capable of impressive, sometimes amazing, acts of fidelity and devotion."

A. S., *"Paris Notes"*

A young antelope rests across from Schweitzer's room on a mound of fresh manioc leaves brought by women from the jungle for the tame antelopes.

TELEGRAM: JUNE 25, 1953

THE FUNDAMENTAL PRINCIPLE OF MORALITY IS RESPECT FOR LIFE. GOOD IS: TO KNOW PITY, TO HELP OTHERS CONSERVE THEIR LIFE, AND TO SPARE THEM SUFFERING. EVIL IS: TO IGNORE COMPASSION AND TO FAIL TO BE INVOLVED WITH ALL KINDS OF CREATURES, TO CAUSE THEM TO SUFFER AND TO DIE. THE MYSTERIOUS FEELING OF RESPECT FOR LIFE AWAKENS IN US WHEN, IN MEDITATION UPON OURSELVES AND THE WORLD, WE REACH TRUE UNDERSTANDING OF OURSELVES. IT BRINGS US TO DEVOTE OURSELVES TO OTHER CREATURES AND TO RECOGNIZE, THEREFORE, THOSE MOMENTS OF REJOICING WHICH TRANSFORM US IN OUR PILGRIMAGE ON EARTH.

ALBERT SCHWEITZER

43

Against opposition from workers and staff, Schweitzer rescues an orange tree from being cut down to make room for a roadway near the last of the new buildings, a ward for patients. When the foundation of the building was dug, he saved some of the rich black earth for the tree. Because the tree was preserved, cars cannot drive full-circle in the compound. To Schweitzer, the tree seemed more important.

"A tree grows, bears fruit—then, after a certain time, it no longer grows, it loses its leaves, its branches wither. What happens? Why is its vital energy checked? Because it did not sink deep enough roots into the earth on which it stands. Anyone who has to do with trees knows what I mean. The same thing—I thought to myself—has happened with us humans. Humanity has not had deep enough roots. It has not found sustenance and fresh impetus, because the ethical code on which it was based was too narrow and did not have a deep foundation. It has concerned itself only with human beings and our relations with human beings. It has given only a passing nod to our relationship with other living creatures, looking upon it as a nice bit of sentimentality, quite innocuous but of no great significance. But it did have significance. For only if we have an ethical attitude in our thinking about all living creatures does our humanity have deep roots and a rich flowering that cannot wither." A. S.

In the hospital plantation are tall palm-nut trees behind dwarf palms which Schweitzer grew after the men refused to climb the tall trees. Beyond are a thousand fruit trees which he and his workers planted. Schweitzer is intensely proud of his fruit plantation, today the only large one in the Gabon. The yield is heavy, and Schweitzer says: "All can take what they please and there is no longer such a crime as stealing."

"The morality we have lived by was fragmentary only. We must abandon it in favor of the complete, all-embracing love expressed in 'reverence for all life.' That fragmentary moral of concern for human life alone was like a single tone floating in the air, incomplete because the base tone to produce the harmony was missing. Reverence for life gives us the full chord, the harmony. The roots of the philosophy of reverence for life are big and strong, deeply planted, so that the tree can grow without being hurt by storms."   A. S.

From a speech at
Brussels on receipt of the
Lemaire Prize, 1959

"Formerly, people said: Who is your neighbor? Man. Today we must no longer say that. We have gone further and we know that all living beings on earth who strive to maintain life and who long to be spared pain—all living beings on earth are our neighbors." A. S.

Penci (short for Penicillin) gets some scraps from her friend.

He is gentle with all creatures. Thekla, the wild pig, slept as a young animal on Schweitzer's porch. Often she refused to go to sleep until he knelt down, adjusted her "pillow," and sang Brahms' "Lullaby." When he practiced on his pedal-piano at night, he often had an animal for audience—an antelope, a chimp, or parrot.

With no one but Schweitzer will the pelican venture so close.

WITH REGARD TO EXPERIMENTS CARRIED OUT ON ANIMALS

Those who test medicines or operating techniques on animals or who inoculate them with illnesses in order to help mankind through the results they hope to obtain in this way must never quiet their conscience with the general excuse that in practicing these cruel methods they are pursuing a lofty purpose.

In every individual case they must ascertain whether it is really necessary to impose such a sacrifice on the animal for the sake of humanity. They should take a very particular care to reduce suffering as much as is within their power.

How many crimes are committed in laboratories where anesthesia is often omitted to save time or trouble! How many more are committed when animals are subjected to torture merely to demonstrate to students things long known to be facts! Precisely because the animal has, by serving in the realm of experimentation, made it possible for such precious information to be obtained for suffering humanity—but at the cost of its pain—a new bond of solidarity has been created between the animal and us.

Each of us has, as a result, the obligation to do as much good for these creatures as he can. When I come to the aid of an insect in distress, I am doing nothing more than trying to pay a part of the forever-renewed debt of man to beast.

Prepared by Albert Schweitzer
in response to a request from
groups in the United States, 1962

Inspector General
Bureau of Hunting
Ministry of France Overseas
27 Rue Oudinot

Dear Sir:

For the last eighteen months I have been keeping a young female gorilla a native brought me when it was only eight or ten days old. With a great deal of care we have been able to keep it alive. I had declared the animal immediately to the local agent of the forestry service.

At about the same time someone brought to me a small male chimpanzee, the lower part of whose legs were completely paralyzed. We have been equally successful in keeping him alive, and his paralysis has slowly decreased.

Since I have been able, thanks to the devoted care of my staff, to save the lives of these two little creatures, I take my courage in both hands and appeal to your benevolent good will for permission to keep them for a while. I would like to keep the gorilla in order to present it eventually to the Natural History Museum of Paris. Professor Urbain has been informed of my intention and he would be delighted to have the animal.

As for the chimpanzee, I would like to present it to the Zoological Gardens in Basle, in recognition of the exceedingly generous support that the people of Basle have given my hospital over the years.

I would be deeply grateful if you could grant this request and inform me what forms must be filled out in order to take the little gorilla to Paris and to bring the chimpanzee to Basle. How much will I have to pay the Forestry Service to reimburse it for the chimpanzee?

Please accept, Monsieur l'Inspecteur-General, assurances of my high regard.

Yours devotedly,
Albert Schweitzer

I, the undersigned, Albert Schweitzer, do hereby certify that I am presenting to Mr. Byron W. Bernard, representing the Zoological Gardens in Cincinnati, Ohio, a two-year-old female gorilla, which I was authorized by the Waters and Forests Service to raise when it was brought sick to me as an infant.

Albert Schweitzer

The chimps Romeo and Juliet are inseparable. Their companion is Verena, a Swiss nurse.

Rhena Schweitzer Eckert, like her father, loves animals, and like him makes friends with animals who are shy with others.

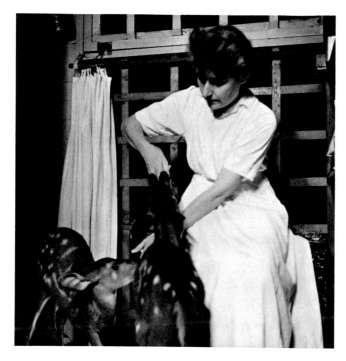

Ali Silver, a Dutch nurse and trusted aide, takes special care of the sick animals. In her room sleep an antelope and several dogs. Each morning, after the first bell, she visits the goat stable for sick call, disinfects and bandages any wounds.

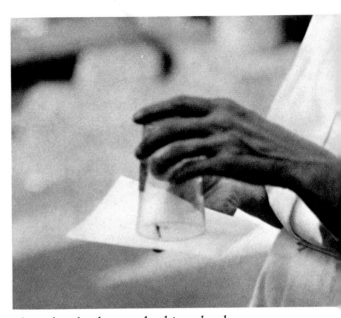

"ALI, THE GOOD LORD CALLS."

Ali, the Dutch nurse who is one of Schweitzer's chief assistants, catches a bee that has wandered into the pharmacy with a piece of cardboard and a glass to release it outside. Reverence for life is practised for even the smallest and most troublesome creatures. "I always think that an angel whispers to the good Lord that one of his creatures has been saved," Schweitzer says.

A sign of painted ducks and chickens warns drivers to go slowly.

52

Schweitzer found Sizi after he heard crying one day and insisted on ripping up the boards of the floor to locate it. A kitten lay below; no one knew how it got there.

"We must be men of the future who allow their hearts to speak along with their reason. Only then will we develop into what we are meant to be: not supermen but real men, living and acting in the spirit of profound humanism." A. S., "*Brussels Notes*"

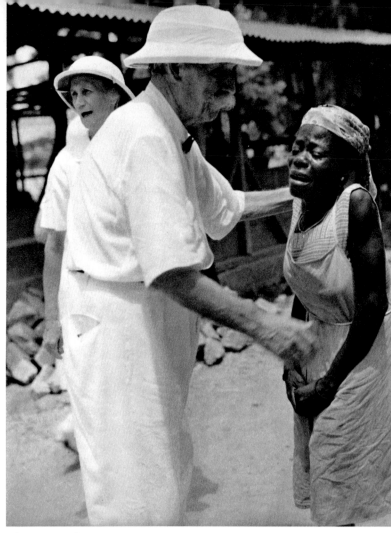

Schweitzer comforts a woman who was crying because others made fun of her hunched back. He said in anger, "If anyone laughs at her again, he will have to leave the hospital!"

SKETCH OF AN ARTICLE FOR A YEARBOOK FOR THE GERMAN WAR BLIND, 1957

As pastor and doctor I have been able to gain insight into the great problem faced by those who have been denied the light of the eye or who have lost it. I have been moved by the way in which many of these persons have succeeded in triumphing over this fate. I have met blind persons who, through the peace that emanated from them, have become a blessing to those around them and to those they encountered. The struggle to cope with this condition is an especially difficult one for the war blind in every nation. We who have suffered no such hardships, or only minor ones, must sometimes feel embarrassed because we are so much better off, and we must bring to them more than the ordinary compassion. Those who have had to endure what we have been spared have a right to have us treat them with a constant understanding and kindly readiness to help.   A. S.

"The idea of humanism was born in antiquity, beginning with the prophecies of Jesus in the Beatitudes, where he speaks of those who are merciful who will obtain mercy, of those who seek peace and who are God's children."   A. S., *"Brussels Notes."*

Written by Schweitzer in concrete pillars at the entrance to the hospital are the words of the Beatitudes: Blessed are the merciful, for they shall obtain mercy. Blessed are the peacemakers, for they shall be called the children of God.

 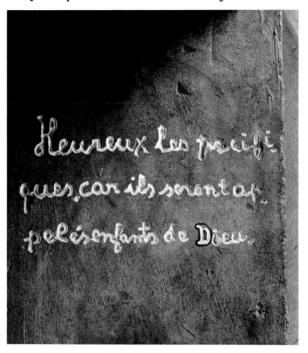

On the stretcher is a man who had recently been a patient and had stolen medicine from the hospital. When he returned by boat, seriously hurt in an accident, Schweitzer was urged not to receive him. He ordered that he be taken to the operating room immediately.

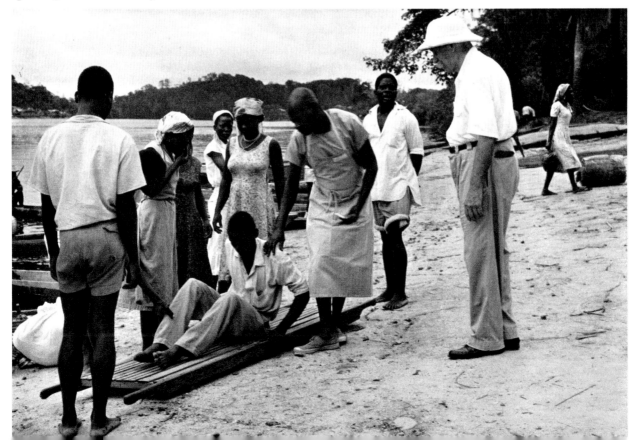

"Let the time be dictated by its ripening." A. S.

THE CYCLE OF LIFE: BEGINNINGS

In Schweitzer's small blue notebooks, carried in his hip pocket, the evidence of the varied activities of the days accumulates. Here is the record of the cycle of days, the elemental life of the hospital village, reflecting the diverse yet orderly pattern of nature's ways. Here is a note about the birth of a child or a baby antelope, the arrival of rice, the sketch for a building in the leper village, the death of a patient. Life is not random but predictable in its rituals, not broken but continuous, a permanent reality. Both the variety and the steady monotony of nature are reflected in Schweitzer's own rhythms.

Birth is the beginning and a time for celebration. Many women who, in the years before, gave birth attended only by old women of the village come now to the hospital for delivery. Earlier, many women and children died in the process of birth. The old women advised the young not to see a doctor, telling them it would bring bad luck. Schweitzer countered the suggestion by a simple tactic. He gave every baby born at the hospital a little bonnet and dress. The parents were full of pleasure that a new baby should receive such a gift. A doctor now means good luck.

Twins (who are considered a bad omen and therefore unwelcome at home) and orphans are raised in the hospital nursery, La Pouponniere. They grow up and enjoy a normal childhood, with many foster parents; a number stay at the hospital helping at small tasks, running messages, picking fruit, and going to school at the Catholic and Protestant missions nearby.

Just as birth is a cause for celebration, so too the anniversary of birth is a great day at the hospital. Early on the festive morning, everyone gathers outside the room of the one whose birthday it is to sing an old German hymn, *Herr, harre meiner Seele*—"Lord, wait for my soul"—then everyone files into the room to shake hands and congratulate him. At breakfast, three lighted candles and green sprigs may decorate his plate. Homemade presents from the staff are piled beside—perhaps an elephant carved in ivory or a painted grass mat. Two eggs, a rare treat, are brought in—one, by tradition from the times when eggs were scarce, to be shared with someone else.

At lunch the "birthday child" may select his own menu (Schweitzer on his own chooses a ritual meal of his favorite Alsatian dishes: onion soup, *quiche lorraine*, fruit for dessert). After the meal, Schweitzer raps on his cup and makes a speech to the honored guest. To one such he said: "I hope you will remember the awakening in the morning, the singing for the *Geburtstags Kind*, the birthday child; keep it in your heart."

All these rituals and celebrations—like the Easter eggs and gifts, the Christmas carols and pageant—vary the patterns of the days and give emphasis to the continuity of life in a hospital that is more than a hospital—a community and a family. "Traditions are disappearing in the world today," Schweitzer says. "What a great pity! The world cannot do without traditions."

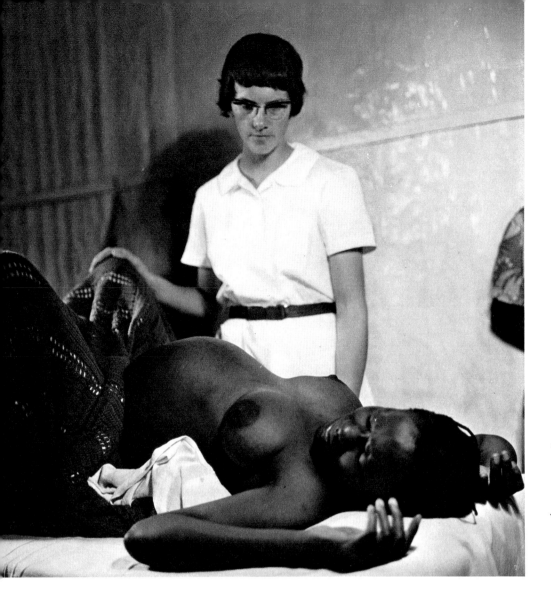

Jacqueline, the daughter of a workman who came to the hospital as a leper in 1927, came from her home in Libreville to have her first child. The nurse Joan is from the Netherlands.

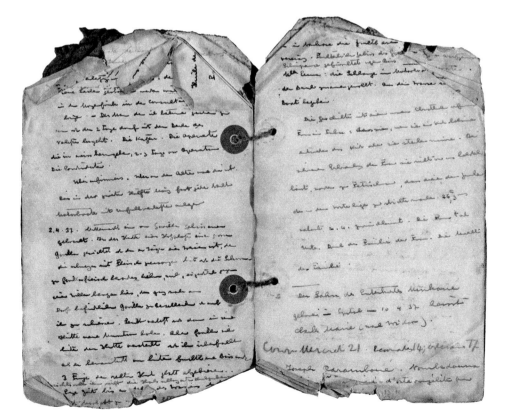

"1937, HEFT FÜR KLEINE NOTIZEN. IN TASCHE TRAGEN."
("Notebook for little notes. To be carried in the pocket.")

Pages from the blue-covered notebooks which Schweitzer carries in his hip pocket. The pages of the homemade notebooks are threaded together with fishing line—just as his manuscripts are. Into these daily journals, written in French and German, goes the record of life at Lambarene. In these pages for 1937 he writes of a patient who had an encounter with a gorilla, of a snake found in a boat, and the birth of a baby—named for Charles Marie Widor, Schweitzer's organ teacher.

Acte de baptême. Esquisse

Ce trois mai 1956 fut baptisé à Lambaréné Gabon (Afrique Equatoriale Française) Lothar Alexander de Rosen, né le huit janvier 1956 à Pointe-Noire, fils de Gustave Friedrich Baron von Rosen, domicilié à Pointe-Noire, né le quatre février 1924 à Eyckholm (Estland), et de Gisela née Muransky, son épouse, née le deux avril 1926 à Riga. Mariage civil le dix-neuf avril 1953 à Laaken (près Hannover); mariage religieux à Lauenburg près Hamburg, le deux mai 1953. Parrain: Hans Baron von Rosen, domicilié à ... Représenté par Mme Hanna Obermann (Lambaréné). Marraine: Mme Edeltraut Hornbach habitant Hambourg, Représentée par Mme Edeltraut Lucks Albertine van Beek-Vollenhoven (Lambaréné). Le baptême est célébré par Albert Schweitzer, pasteur de l'Eglise de la Confession d'Augsburg d'Alsace.
Lambaréné le trois mai 1956: Albert Schweitzer

Certificate for a child baptized at Lambarene in 1956

BAPTISMAL STATEMENT

We wish this child to be baptized so that he may be a member of the Christian Church.

Throughout his life he should know and always remember that he belongs to the Christian Church and through it to our Lord Jesus. He must wish to live as a Christian by letting himself be guided by the spirit of Jesus.

The words and the spirit of Jesus must be the light on the road of his life.

The ceremony of baptism means, first, that his parents and those who have agreed to be his godparents wish to rear him in the spirit of Christ. God grant that he find in his life those persons who will show him the way to Jesus and who will lead him along this path. May he recognize the simple and profound Christian piety that consists in knowing that we must be in this world without being of this world. For we are summoned to belong to another world, the eternal and spiritual world from which we come and to which we return when we have fulfilled our earthly pilgrimage.

God give his grace to this infant, guarding his heart and soul while he lives, and the will to be his child.

And we, each time that we assist in a baptism, may we remember that we also have been baptized, and that we also have been called to be children of God. A. S.

Günsbach
August 7, 1954

"Start early to instill in your students awareness that they are on this earth to help and serve others, that is as important to pass on to them as knowledge." A. S.

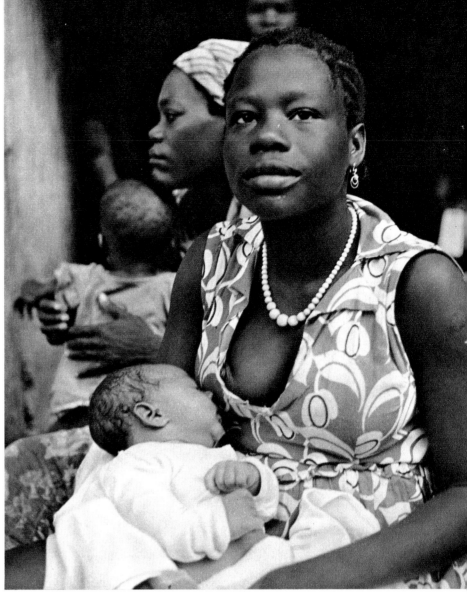

Gifts from friends abroad sustain the hospital. "Something has to happen in someone's heart before anything happens in Lambarene." A. S.

Dr. Isao Takahashi, a Japanese, and his wife, who supervises the kitchen in Lambarene, arrived a few years ago. When asked why he had come, he said, "We have come to serve." He had worked with leper colonies in the Far East; he and his wife are in charge of the leper village at the jungle hospital.

The hospital nursery-orphanage, La Pouponniere, is in charge of Mama Helene, who has served almost 35 years and is now going blind.

I sit here at my desk today, Palm Sunday morning, and think, while I do this and that, about your confirmation and mine.

I was confirmed on Palm Sunday at Mülhouse and the state of my feelings on that day of celebration still lives vividly in my memory. Now today is your own confirmation. Your life is not, as mine was at that time, untroubled by pain and sorrow. You have experienced both since childhood and you have become older, thereby, than your years would indicate.

May God let you experience joy in the coming years! You are confirmed and have made the decision to walk through life as a child of God. May you be serious in this always! For in this lies true happiness. Remain true to yourself and to Jesus! Seek always for the essential of religion, for that which is the evangel, that is, according to the Gospel of Jesus. All other things come second after this.

Read for yourself in the New Testament; do not give it up as long as you live, for in this you will learn what the spirit of Jesus is. The wonderful sayings will light you on your way. And hold to the Church! Do not let Sunday be taken from you, either through sports activities or through anything else. If your soul has no Sunday, it becomes an orphan. And when you get lost in life, know that the road of return to God is always open. God watch over you. Be a help to your mother, who has had to endure so many hardships. If you can be active in the service of religion, do not let the opportunity go by. Keep your eyes open to see where God needs you, to help him in love, in which we belong to him.

Now church will be over and you all walk through the spring sunshine to your home. I will be with you in my thoughts this whole day.

From my heart, your godfather,
Albert Schweitzer

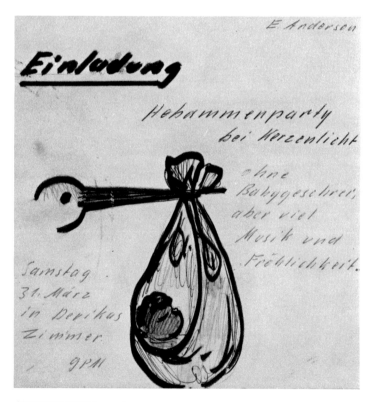

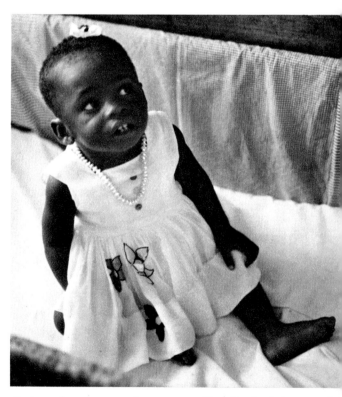

AN INVITATION
"*Party by candlelight given by the midwives, without babies crying but with much music and gaiety, Saturday, May 31, 1960, in Devika's room, 9 P.M.*"

Susie at the party, on the occasion of her first birthday. Susie's mother, a Gabonese, had committed suicide, and before dying had asked an English nurse, Joan Clent, to care for her child. The nurse adopted the baby.

THE CYCLE OF LIFE: ENDINGS

Whenever a new member of the hospital staff arrives in Lambarene, a large bronze bell is rung. It rings again when one departs, for the cycle of life has its endings as well as its beginnings, and for every greeting and meeting there is a farewell. And for every farewell there comes a new beginning. "Time is my enemy," Schweitzer says, aware of the advance of age and the work still to be done. But he has been too busy to brood over time gone: "When I see girls who were born here coming back to the hospital to have babies of their own, that is the only time I know I am growing old."

Just as there are rituals at the hospital for birth, and for the anniversary of birth, so too there is the ritual of farewell. On the last evening, a special song of farewell, "Au Revoir," is sung by leper children, and the next morning Schweitzer and the staff go down to the landing to see the visitors or staff off. But, though there are many such farewells, each time it is hard to say good-by. After one such departure, Schweitzer turned away to walk by himself. "After a farewell, one wishes to be alone."

Some of the farewells are not good-by, for many friends return. But some are lasting; death, too, is part of the continuity and rhythm of life. Outside the window of Schweitzer's room, under a palm tree in the tall grass, stand two crosses that represent such farewells. One marks the grave of Helene Schweitzer, his wife, who died in 1957 in Zurich after many years of struggle against illness. The other is that of Mlle. Emma Hausknecht, his loyal associate for thirty years, who died in 1956 in Strasbourg. Their ashes were brought home to Lambarene where the center of their life had been.

When asked about the possibility of life after death, Schweitzer replied: "No one knows. But as long as someone is kept alive in the heart, he is alive." For those who grieve, he says, as he did in a letter to a friend: "There is nothing for us to do but to seek the consolation of grieving with those who grieve, to devote ourselves to helping them in their misfortune, and to make them realize that the love which God has put in the hearts of men is a living reality."

A hospital is dedicated to the preservation of life and the prevention of pain, but not every life can be saved and not all pain can be avoided. As Schweitzer watched autumn leaves drift slowly to earth in Günsbach, he mused: "People should be allowed to die that way—naturally, easily, without pain." And when his favorite pelican died, he said: "He didn't have to suffer. *Scheiden ohne Leiden*—to part without suffering—is always beautiful." For life even in death may have beauty, a harmonious place in the nature of things. Life renews itself everywhere.

"I dare not answer this question. As a physician I can say that I know of people in despair who, for reasons of health, or when their mind is ill, desire to end their lives. We should not judge this as right or wrong. But sometimes people kill themselves because they have found no one to help them. They have lost hope in mankind. They have found no compassion. When we are truly filled with the idea of reverence for life, all our attitudes, thinking, actions change. We must go deep into ourselves to find inspiration. Slogans, publicity, and means of communication don't help us to find this philosophy. Nor is there one formula for everyone. But if we turn within, pondering our duty in this world in silence, and act to move toward this goal, a change will come about. There are many opportunities to prove that we live in the spirit of the philosophy of 'reverence for life.'"
Copenhagen, 1959

Between the leper village and the hospital is a small Moslem cemetery, given by Schweitzer to the Moham- medans, whom the Gabonese do not like to receive into their own burial grounds. Once every year Moslems come to thank Schweitzer for this kindness. Nearby is another cemetery—for those who have died at the hospital and have no family burial ground.

"You see, when I get to Europe, my first duty is to those I don't find any more. Gradually there are more of those whose graves I visit than those I still find. Gradually, gradually there are fewer and fewer of those who shared my youth with me."   A. S.

When in Europe Schweitzer always went first to visit the graves of friends. "It always seems to me, when I visit their graves, that they know it."

Near Schweitzer's window, where he can look out and see them as he works at his desk, are two crosses marking the graves of his wife, Helene, who died in 1957, and his nurse and associate Mlle. Emma Hausknecht, who died in 1956. He himself carved the words on them; as he did so he said, "The third cross I am carving for myself."

LETTER TO A LIEUTENANT (JG) IN THE UNITED STATES
NAVY WHO WAS ON HIS WAY TO KOREA

Lambarene, December 27, 1952

Your letter has moved me deeply. You express the hopelessness we all experience in this terrible time.

Forgive me for not having answered you at once. I was traveling. My life is a very difficult one. I cannot master all the things, all the work I should be doing. And I did not want to let someone else write to you. I wanted to write you myself. I believe that there is reason for hope. Hope is there like a small band of light on the sky before the sunrise. There begins to stir in the world a new spirit, a spirit of humanity. The terrible thing was that we fell into inhumanity without knowing it. And because the new spirit begins to stir there is hope, for the spirit is the great transforming power.

This is what the great ones, the prophets, Jesus and Paul have told us. So we will profess that spirit and proclaim it. Revolution is an evil word, for it means that something new is to come through destruction. Good never comes through destruction, that we have seen in all revolutions—they bring good only intermingled with evil. Never talk of revolutions. It is the spirit that works. To create means evolution. All in it is positive. Nothing is negative. The spirit teaches us the great truth that we men must come to love, that is to have reverence for life, to true humanity. So, you and I and so many others, men in whom that spirit is alive and active, will teach, experience, and affirm this with confidence in the power of the spirit.

I would indeed be happy to help you find hope in your despair, for we need hope to live. My thoughts will follow you in Korea. Send me news of you. The simplest way is to address your letters to Dr. Albert Schweitzer, Günsbach, Alsace, France. They will be forwarded from there to me in Africa.

God bless you, dear brother,

Affectionately,
Albert Schweitzer

"When I hear a baby's cry of pain change into a normal cry of hunger, to my ears that is the most beautiful music—and there are those who say I have good ears for music." A. S.

On their way home after the birth of their daughter, one couple came to thank the doctor and say good-by. Schweitzer kissed the baby's hand and said to her mother, "Tell her some day that I was her first admirer. It was here that she had her first night and her first dreams."

"Way back, the Schweitzers were cowherds and servants. They were always people who served." A. S.

III
THE MINISTRY
OF
SERVICE

Schweitzer has been a renowned Biblical scholar and has studied and meditated upon the life of Jesus as few have ever done. But the Bible's profoundest lesson seemed to him a simple one: that "he who would find his life must lose it," and he who would follow as a disciple must become a servant of men.

In obedience to the command to serve, he created a hospital village and a leper village in the Gabon, French Equatorial Africa. He became a doctor of medicine to relieve men's suffering; he became a builder as well, for in order to heal in the jungle a hospital had to be constructed where none was. The strong, expressive hands that had brought beauty from the greatest organs of Europe and wisdom from his pen, now used with skill the hoe and the pruning shears; the tools of building—the level, the hammer, and the saw; and the instruments of surgery—the scalpel and needle.

From the first operations in a whitewashed chicken coop in 1913 to the village hospital of seventy-two buildings a half-century later, more than 100,000 patients have passed through the clinic. Today it houses 500 patients and their relatives at a time, and the number treated grows each year. Word of the hospital community has spread throughout the Gabon. Many come now for modern medical care who had depended in the past on fetishes and superstition.

Doctors and nurses from many countries serve on the staff, with the assistance of several dozen Gabonese. The young doctors perform the surgery for which *le grand Docteur* no longer trusted his hands after his seventieth birthday, as his eyesight grew less sharp. Many others, who cannot give more than a few weeks or months, come during vacations to put their medical skills to work.

Others arrive to build, to drive the truck and jeep, to haul concrete and bananas, and to work together with the families of patients on the constant job of construction, repair, and maintenance of roads and buildings. Schweitzer no longer climbs the scaffolding, but he still carries water from the river and pushes a wheelbarrow and drives a straight nail. All the buildings are erected to his own specifications, adapted from the advice of native carpenters—from east to west in an elongated pattern, so that the sun passing overhead does not strike the sides—and each room has cross ventilation. The walls on the long sides are made of mosquito netting, open to the breezes, and windows in other walls are screened against insects. Schweitzer constructs a double ceiling for all rooms, shutting out extreme temperatures, a lesson learned from organ lofts. He has accepted the given facts of terrain and climate and suited the buildings to them.

This is a community where life is lived simply, where the plumbing is elementary and electricity is available only for the X-ray machine and the lights of the operating room. The atmosphere is more that of a cheerful African village than of a hospital. Gabonese in colorful dress roam the streets, women nurse their babies among the animals whose home this also is. Schweitzer insists that automobiles not be driven into the compound. Nailing up a parking sign just outside the plantation, he threatens, only partly in jest, "I will strew nails around if people don't obey!"

There is an earthy simplicity in Schweitzer's attitude toward all things. As he walks about, picking up the stones needed in the making of concrete for his buildings, he says: "Two things make me rich in Gabon, one is stones of all sizes, the other is the compost heap. Why do you think we have so many animals? To do what comes naturally!" For he is peasant and farmer as well as builder, scholar, and physician, and his only show of pride comes when he views his abundant garden and fruitful plantation. With joy he performs tree surgery and grafting and carries antelope droppings to fertilize the roots. For Schweitzer the life of service knows no menial chores.

TO THE STUDENTS OF A SCHOOL FOR NURSES WHO ASKED ME FOR A MOTTO

Lambarene, February 20, 1953

You ask me to give you a motto. Here it is: SERVICE. Let this word accompany each of you throughout your life. Let it be before you as you seek your way and your duty in the world. May it be recalled to your minds if ever you are tempted to forget it or to set it aside. It will not always be a comfortable companion but it will always be a faithful one. And it will be able to lead you to happiness, no matter what the experiences of your lives are. Never have this word on your lips, but keep it in your hearts. And may it be a confidant that will teach you not only to do good but to do it simply and humbly.

My good wishes to you
Albert Schweitzer

"The three islands in the Ogowe River near the village Igendja, forty-eight miles downriver from the Lambarene hospital, where at sunset, on a day in September 1915, there flashed upon my mind unforeseen and unsought the knowledge that the idea of reverence for life is the basic principle of goodness." A. S.

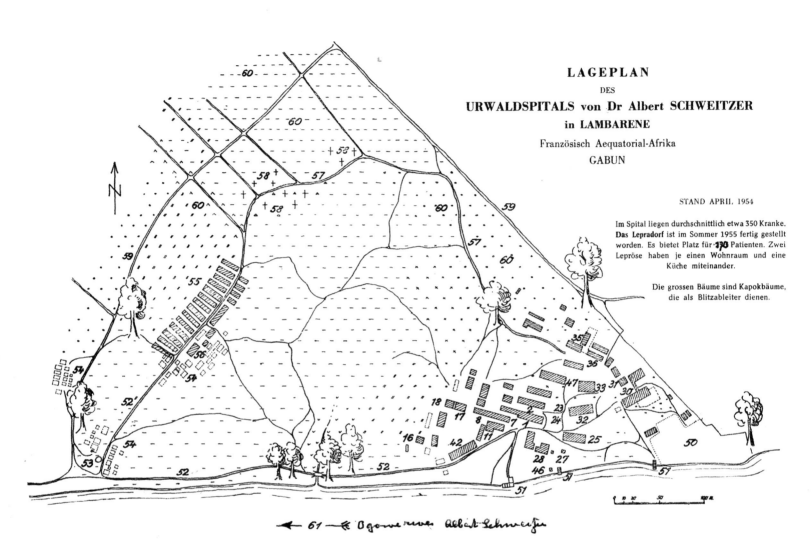

LAGEPLAN

DES

URWALDSPITALS von Dr Albert SCHWEITZER

in LAMBARENE

Französisch Aequatorial-Afrika

GABUN

STAND APRIL 1954

Im Spital liegen durchschnittlich etwa 350 Kranke. **Das Lepradorf** ist im Sommer 1955 fertig gestellt worden. Es bietet Platz für 170 Patienten. Zwei Lepröse haben je einen Wohnraum und eine Küche miteinander.

Die grossen Bäume sind Kapokbäume, die als Blitzableiter dienen.

1 Untersuchungs- und Operationsräume
2 Operierte Kranke
7 Lebensmittelvorratsräume
8 Kranke aus dem fernen Innern des Landes
11 Schwerkranke Eingeborene
16 Bau für lärmende Geisteskranke
17 Bau für ruhige Geisteskranke
18 Anatomie
23 Grosses Wasserreservoir

24 Glocke
25 Haus für europäische Kranke
27 Brunnen
28 Bootsschuppen und Reparaturwerkstatt
30 Wohnhaus der europäischen Kranken
31 Küche und Vorratshäuser
32 Wohnhaus für europäische Helfer
33 Gemeinsamer Essaal
35 Ställe und Ökonomiegebäude

36 Ställe und Ökonomiegebäude
42 Haus für Schwerkranke
46 Brunnen für die trockene Jahreszeit
47 Haus Sans-Souci
50 Gemüsegarten
51 Anlegestellen für Schiffe und Boote
52 Unterer Weg zum Leprösendorf
53 Brunnen der Leprösensiedlung
54 Die ersten primitiven Leprösenbehausungen

55 Das neue Leprösendorf
56 Haus « Greta Lagerfelt »
57 Oberer Weg zum Leprösendorf
58 Friedhof
59 Waldstrasse
60 Obstbaumpflanzungen
61 Ogowefluss

A recent map of the hospital, showing some of the newer buildings (approximately eight others have been erected since Schweitzer marked this map). The Ogowe River is noted in his handwriting.

"Thank the Lord for He is friendly, and His kindness is everlasting." A. S., *grace at meals*

THE PATTERN OF THE DAYS

The pattern of the days at the hospital, like the rhythms of nature, is related to need. It is orderly. "We live simply," Schweitzer says. "No one needs a watch. A watch wouldn't last long in the heat and humidity anyway. The day's activities are separated by the gong. A bell tells you when it is time to eat or time to work." For everything there is a season, and a time for everything under the sun.

Bells have a special meaning for Schweitzer. It was the bell of his church in Günsbach that rang into his heart as a child *Thou shalt not kill* when he was hunting birds with a boyhood friend. He remembers also that those same bells rang on the Good Friday when he left for Africa. The bells are a symbol of both order and beauty; within their music is the harmony of the days.

At 5:30 in the morning at Lambarene the crickets chirp in the darkness, and as the reveille gong is sounded at 6:30 the dawn begins. At 7:30 it sounds for breakfast, the most informal meal of the day. At 8 it calls everyone to work. All patients who are to receive medicine or have their dressings renewed assemble before the main hospital building. At 12 the gong signals the close of morning work, and at 12:30 the call to lunch. The staff meets in the dining hall and the patients, who have earlier received their rations of bananas, rice, manioc, and palm oil, prepare their own meals on their family fires under the red roofs of the wards.

The staff lunch begins with grace: "Danket dem Herrn denn er ist freundlich und seine Gute wahret ewiglich." Then a bowl of homemade soup, a plate of home-grown fruits and green salad, freshly baked bread, and butter twice a week. After lunch, siesta, and then the gong rings again at 2 for the work of the afternoon. At 5:30 it rings for the close of the working day. At 7 it sounds for dinner and the staff gathers at the table, lit now by the soft yellow glow of the kerosene lamps. After dinner, Schweitzer moves to the ancient, rickety piano, too loyal to it to use the new one beside it. He plays a hymn as the others sing, then reads from the Bible each night in German and in French, interpreting and inviting comment as he goes along. It is a peaceful end of a busy, exhausting day.

Schweitzer returns to his room, but after the 9 o'clock curfew is struck on the bronze bell to signal time for quiet on the hospital grounds, his light often shines behind his curtains after midnight as he works on his correspondence, his manuscripts, or a Bach score.

Just as the day is ordered, so too is the week. Every day is laundry day. Ironing is done twice a week; operations, except in emergency, are scheduled for Tuesdays, Thursdays, and Saturdays. On Wednesdays and Thursdays the truck arrives with bananas. Saturday is cleaning day and payday. After the evening meal on Saturday, the staff listens to a concert of music on the victrola, while the rest of the hospital relaxes in singing native songs. Sunday is the seventh day, a time for rest, for worship, and for meditation. And a new week has begun.

"First think, then do." A. S.

THE IMPORTANCE OF WORK

For Schweitzer work is necessary to the preservation of life itself. Usefulness is the test of value; that which sustains life is good. "Beauty is nothing; usefulness is everything," he said when a friend apologized to him for mending a lampshade with scotch tape. He prefers fruit trees to flowers or ornamental trees—because they are useful—and is immensely proud of the orchard of more than a thousand trees he has planted on the hospital grounds: papaya, guava, oranges, grapefruit, mangoes, breadfruit, *pommes de Cythere*.

There is frugality at the hospital, a habit necessary in a jungle where all things taken for granted elsewhere—paper, string, and the like—must be imported. The backs of old letters and envelopes are re-used; string is hoarded to bind notebooks, packages, and manuscripts; luggage tags are transformed into identification tags for the patients. Schweitzer's habits of economy were learned as a child when his grandmother admonished him to save even the stems and cores of apples—the one for the woodbin, the other into the trough with the pigfeed. He likes handmade things because they are made unhurriedly and with care, and his shirts used to be made for him by a Günsbach neighbor. When she died a few years ago, her daughter took over the task. His one black suit, which he wears almost everywhere in Europe, was made by a Günsbach tailor ten years ago. The Prince Albert he wore to give his Nobel Prize address was a relic of his student days, more than forty years old.

Not only because Schweitzer's tastes are simple, but also because machinery is difficult to maintain in the steamy jungle, tasks customarily handled by machine are often performed by hand. Even the communication system is personal rather than mechanical. There is no telephone, and a native boy carries messages about the village. "*You* are my telephone," Schweitzer tells him.

Work is not only necessary but satisfying and fulfilling, Schweitzer believes. Even visitors are encouraged to work. In his copy of Homer's Odyssey, Schweitzer has underlined a passage that says guests should be asked to work, for thereby they become part of the household. Work introduces the stranger to the community, and in participating he becomes a friend. Most of those who stay for any length of time want to share in the hospital's busy activities. "This is the contribution of four students who came for a visit," Schweitzer will say, pointing to a new section of road. One young student of philosophy who came to ask questions remained to break stones for the foundation of a building. Schweitzer told him: "If you choose philosophy for your road, you will find it a stony one. You have to have a strong back, and this is the best way to get one. This is the beginning." Afterwards, in the evening, he talked to him about philosophy.

Even the lepers work at jobs suited to their physical limitations, making mats or paddling the pirogues—both jobs that can be done sitting down. The mentally ill work, too, in the peaceful garden by the river.

Appel, the gong for work, rings after breakfast, and every morning the workers—the healthy members of patients' families—line up in front of Schweitzer's porch and he gives out the assignments for the day. Then, jobs assigned, he sweeps off his white tropical hat, bows to the workers, and says, "Au travail! To work!" "Merci, Docteur," they reply with varying degrees of enthusiasm and depart with hoe, shovel, and hammer to build or repair roads and buildings, to cultivate the orchard and the gardens. Schweitzer is always close at hand, making sure the workers perform their tasks well: "I do not hear the sound of the hammer!" "When I am here small things stay small and big things are dealt with as big—not the other way around."

And if the workers slow down or stop altogether, he reminds them: "Don't you know the Bible? 'In the sweat of thy face shalt thou eat bread.' " "But it's so hot," one responded with logic and humor, "we are sweating already—so why should we need to work?" Schweitzer laughed, but the work went on. He believes in discipline, for others as well as for himself. He asks no one to do what he himself cannot do. Until his eighty-ninth year he worked an hour before breakfast; only now does he begin after breakfast is over, as the others do. When all the workmen have stopped for the day, he can still be found on the building site planning the next day's tasks. "First, think, then do," he will say.

Work, to Schweitzer, is a responsibility to life itself. "Responsibility is a great thing. To shoulder responsibility, not to shirk it. Politically, economically, in so many respects, people in our time don't seem to face their duties. If we learned early in life not to avoid responsibility, the world would look brighter."

Bells summon the hospital village to labor and to rest. The hourly schedule is sounded on chimes made from two railway ties that hang free. An old bell was suspended high in the air and rung by a chain for Sunday services. One day when it sounded furiously at a peculiar time, Horatio, a gorilla, was found swinging from the chain. Today a large bronze bell which Dr. Schweitzer received on his eightieth birthday rings on Sunday and for the arrival and departure of members of the staff. Twice a day a hand bell calls patients to receive their medicines.

Appel has been rung and the work assignments have been given out. Now Schweitzer bows to the workers as they go off for the morning's labor.

Every day is laundry day at the Lambarene hospital. Ironing is done twice a week. Seamstresses make sturdy uniforms and work clothes and mend clothing.

Saturday is cleaning day. Everything is taken from the buildings and scrubbed with cold water and soap and left to dry in the sun—tables, beds, equipment. The old straw used as bedding is thrown out and new straw brought in. All rooms are scrubbed and ceiling cobwebs attacked with long brooms. Every day two bottles of distilled water and two cans of washing water are brought to the staff rooms. Fresh bed linen is supplied every other week and towels (four or five) every week.

Concrete steps lead up from the main hospital street to the other wards or cases.

Schweitzer carries unanswered mail hoping to find time to answer. Mail goes out twice a day and is brought back morning and afternoon in a metal canister, in case of rain, by the hospital village "mailman." Telegrams are delivered immediately and Schweitzer's mail is sent to his room. The rest of the mail is sorted and put at each person's place at the evening meal. The mailman's job is highly valued; he carries his mail in the boat with three men to row him to and from Lambarene.

Under the gentle supervision of Emma Hausknecht, workers tend the vegetable garden. There are cucumbers, spinach, eggplant, tomatoes, radishes, beans, and other vegetables. The garden must be weeded constantly, and the orchard cut back to keep the jungle from encroaching. In the dry season water must be brought from the river to keep the roots in orchard and garden moist.

When the rice supply from Saigon (which used to be the cheapest) became irregular, Schweitzer began to buy bananas from neighboring villages instead. At first they came by boat from up-river, and later a truck was ordered, to carry the huge supply, For the truck a good road was needed. Whereupon Schweitzer, then eighty-seven, and his crew—including four boys from Germany who turned up one day—built an 800-meter road in three months. Since the road had to pass over a small river, he also had to design and build a stone bridge.

Each week it takes eight tons of bananas—large red plantains—to supply the patients and their families, transported twice a week from as far as twenty miles away.

Large supplies of rice are brought to the hospital, particularly in the summer months when there are fewer bananas. Schweitzer meets every shipment with needle and sturdy thread, and when a sack of rice splits at the landing he sews it up on the spot so as not to lose any.

Katharine and Emmy, nurses from Alsace and Switzerland, ladle out the soup which is served each evening. A typical meal might include also fish or crocodile meat, eggplant or another vegetable, crusty French bread baked in the old-fashioned brick oven, and on Saturday evening a cold meal of sausage, fruit, and cheese. At lunch, bowls of fresh fruit such as papaya and avocado are served. For breakfast there are coffee, tea, and cocoa, bread, butter (Thursdays and Saturdays), homemade preserves like Schweitzer's favorite "confiture du grand docteur"—guava fraise—and bitter orange marmalade from their own plantation.

GRACE BEFORE MEALS

Said in Europe: "Mon ame benit le Seigneur et le remercie de tous ses bienfaits. ("My soul blesses the Lord and is grateful to him for all his goodness.")

Said in Africa: "Beni soit l'Eternel car sa misericorde dure eternellement." ("Blessed be God, for his mercy endureth forever.")

"Well, at least I haven't been wasting my time. While I was building, I managed to work out the fingering problem for a difficult Bach cantata." A. S.

Until a truck and jeep came to the hospital, the only vehicle was the wheelbarrow.

Schweitzer's jotted notes of equipment to be bought for him in Europe, and a sketch of measurements for a foundation.

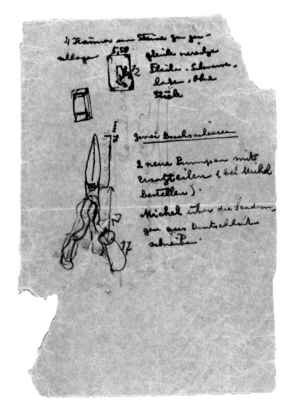

There is no running water at the hospital and the patients' laundry is done at the river bank. Drinking water comes originally from the well and is distilled and filtered several times. Water for other uses—for hospital laundry, dishes, and washing—must be carried up from the river or from a pump run by motor. When it was operated by hand it used to break down frequently and Schweitzer had to fix it several times a week. A Swiss engineer is working on plans for a new, modern system of water supply.

SCHWEITZER'S NOTES FOR AN ORDER OF SUNDAY SERVICE USED IN EUROPE

Divine Service
Singing. Altar. Announcement of hymn. Sermon. Announcement of hymn. At the altar, the
Lord's Prayer. Announcement of divine service at Griesbach at 8 P.M. Closing hymn. Bene-
diction.

Sunday is a day for rest and meditation. A staff member rings the bell that calls all who wish
to come to morning worship. There are two services every Sunday, one in the main hospital
street, the other in the leper village for patients who cannot walk. On a visit to the hospital in
1962, Abbe Pierre of Paris held Sunday mass in the leper village; Schweitzer, attending, sat
among his patients.

This sawn log came by the river, probably drifting from a lumber camp. If no one claims such logs after a few years, Schweitzer and his workers cut them up and use them.

Foundations must be poured in the dry season. Cement is imported, sand is carried from the river's edge. Granite rocks are chipped into gravel by the lepers and other patients.

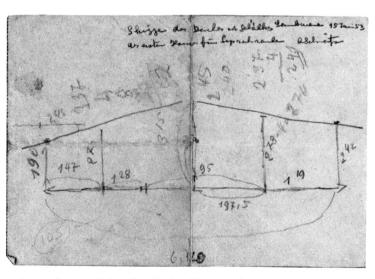

A rough pencil sketch of a building. Schweitzer never uses a detailed plan and rarely even makes a drawing. It reads: "Sketch for the roof and of the construction of the first house for the leper village. A. Schweitzer 15 June '53"

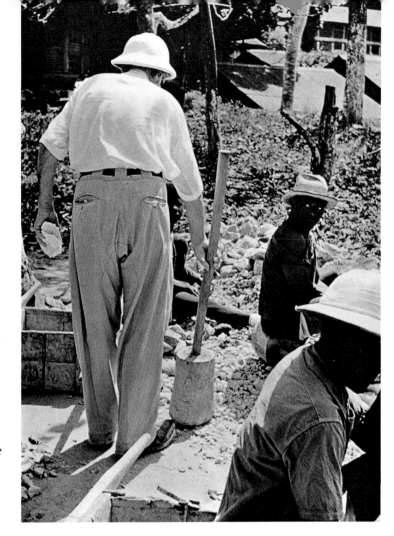

Work on a road: Schweitzer tamps the stones to make a smooth surface.

The joists and beams are jungle mahogany, paduc, manji, or okoume. Village dwellings throughout the Gabon now follow Schweitzer's style of construction. An apprenticeship as one of his carpenters counts for something in the nearby villages.

Emma Hausknecht and others building the kitchen for the leper village.

On the concrete foundations of the huts of the leper village the structure rose. Wood came from the okoume tree, hard and inpervious to termites. When the framework was up, a bamboo lattice was woven with raffia, and palm-leaf shingles bound to the lattice. Protected from the soil by the foundations and from the rain by iron roofs, the walls last for years.

Schweitzer's map-sketch of the leper village and a photograph of the main street. In the leper village, sturdy new buildings have replaced the old bamboo huts which the patients built for themselves. The Nobel Prize money bought the corrugated iron roofs. Two hundred and fifty patients can be accommodated in the village now. Since 1944 the new sulfa drugs have given lepers new hope of cure.

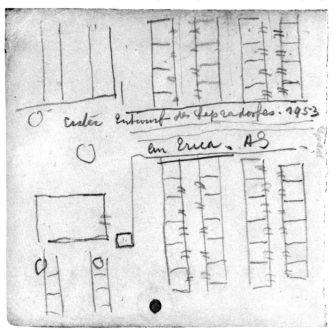

Every morning patients who can walk and who are to receive medication line up at the pharmacy for treatment.

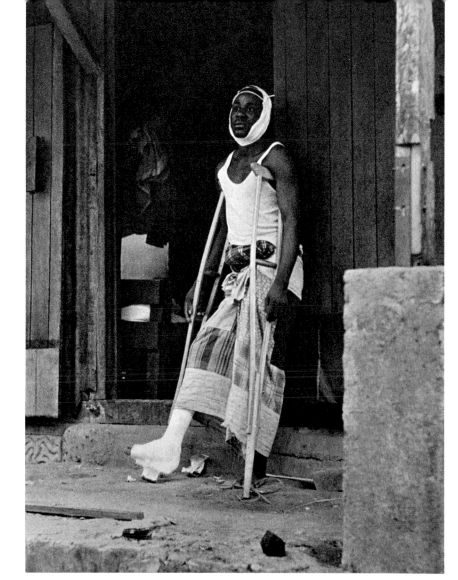

This is a hospital where no one asks, "Are you insured? Can you pay?" Everyone in need is treated without question. Patients who are able pay a normal fee, or in produce—a cock or eggs or a goat.

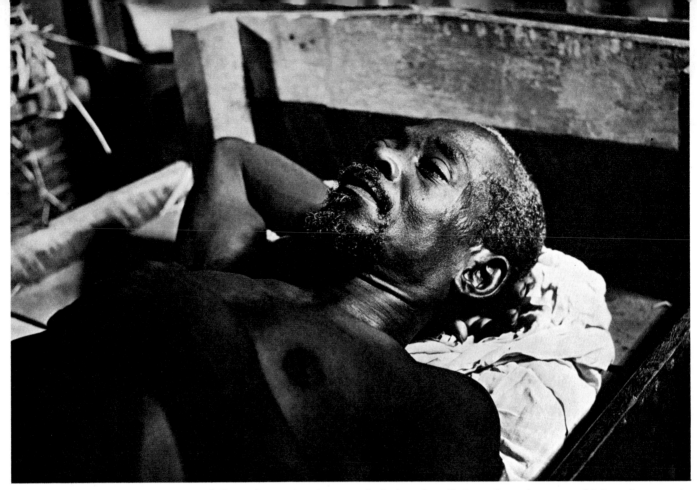

There are wards for European and for Gabonese patients, each designed to fit into the culture to which each group is accustomed. Outside the doors of the Gabonese wards, on the ground, the families who accompany the patients cook their own meals. This hospital custom was initiated when Schweitzer discovered that patients shunned a common kitchen because of their fear of poisoning by members of rival tribes. Private rooms have recently been built for those Gabonese who are accustomed to modern urban living. There are no limited visiting hours, for every day is open house.

Telegram
EMMY MARTIN, GÜNSBACH   SEND TWO NURSES.
JULY 17, SCHWEITZER

IDENTIFICATION TAG FOR PATIENT
Attention: The bearer of this is a patient of Albert Schweitzer and has had to be sent to Brazzaville Hospital for an operation. Please help him in anything he needs.

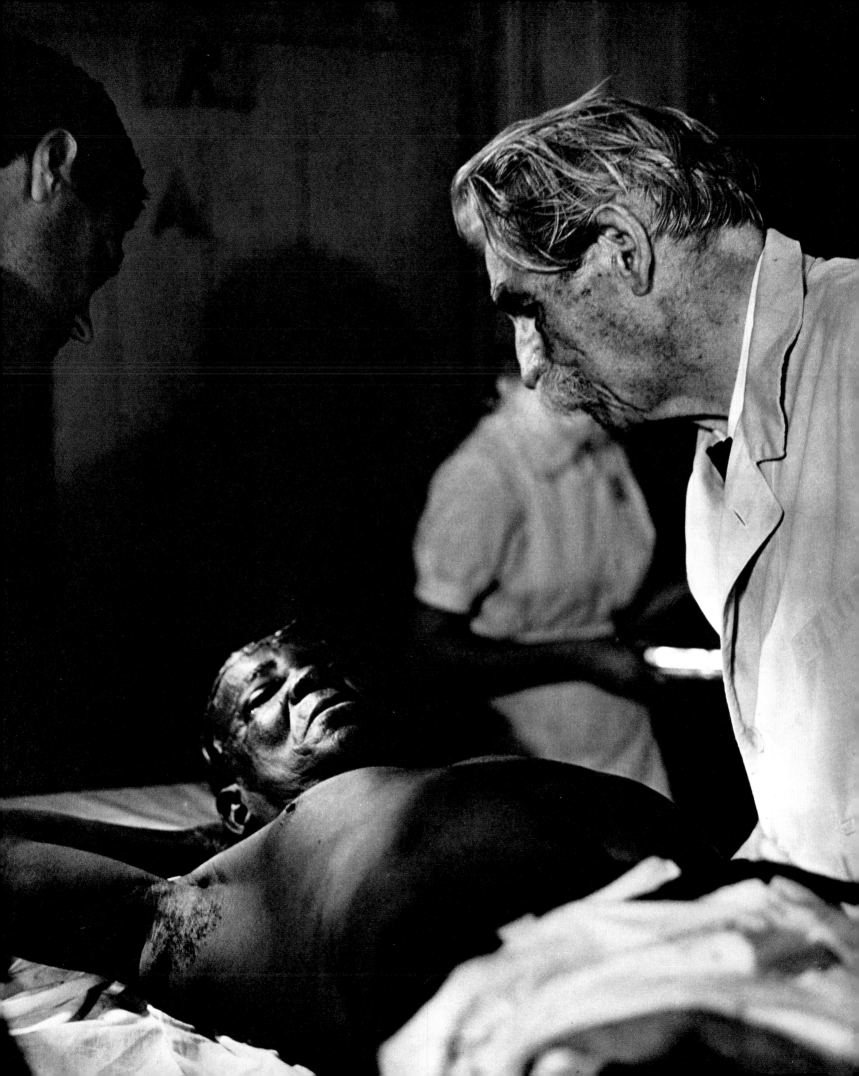

Certificat Médical.

Bulletin d'entrée d'accidenté *traumatisé de bataille*

Je soussigné Albert Schweitzer, Docteur en Médecine, certifie que

le nommé *Detougou Denis*

appartenant à *Maison Mora (Lac Ezangha)*

a été hospitalisé à mon hôpital le *15 juillet 1956*

pour *blessure profonde musculo-cutanée de la main gauche*

(enfau volaire) et section du tendon fléchisseur du troisième

doigt

Le temps d'hospitalisation et une incapacité de travail éventuelle
ne peuvent encore être déterminés.

Ce certificat est délivré pour servir ce que de droit.

Fait à Lambaréné le *quinze juillet 1956*

Albert Schweitzer
Docteur en Médecine.

MEDICAL CERTIFICATE

REPORT ON ADMISSION: *altercation casualty.*

I, THE UNDERSIGNED, *Albert Schweitzer, M.D.,* CERTIFY THAT

NAME: *Detougou, Denis*

BELONGING TO: *Mora residence (Lake Ezangha)*

HAS BEEN HOSPITALIZED IN MY HOSPITAL: *July 15, 1956*

FOR: *deep musculocutaneous wound on the left hand and section of flexor tendon of third finger.*

The period of hospitalization and eventual incapacity for work cannot yet be determined.

This certificate is issued for whomever it may concern.

Lambarene, July 15, 1956

Albert Schweitzer, M.D.

Schweitzer and Ali with Anita, the goat, in the pharmacy. Some of the goats come into the pharmacy to be fed and settle at Schweitzer's feet. As soon as he leaves, they do also. The pharmacy building is the center of the hospital and includes outpatient clinic, operating room, laboratory, delivery room, nursery, X-ray room, dental office, hospital records.

All new patients receive a thorough physical examination. Surgery is often postponed for several weeks while the patient is treated for other ailments such as anemia, malaria, or malnutrition. If transfusions are necessary, members of the patient's family give blood, though it is hard to overcome their fear of doing so.

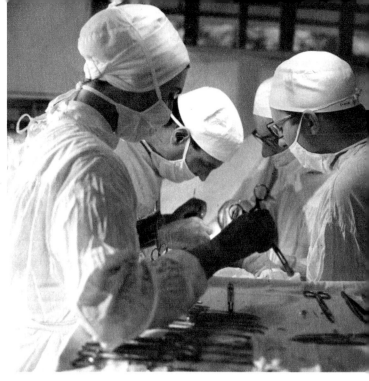

Operations are scheduled three days a week—from morning, if possible, to late afternoon—but emergencies are often necessary. Patients may be kept for several weeks after an operation since adequate nutrition is often not available in their home village and follow-up study almost impossible.

Approximately 1,000 operations are performed each year. There are two modern operating tables and lamps, a good supply of instruments, simple facilities for sterilization. Anesthesia is usually given by spinal injection. Electrical cutting and suction is powered by the large Diesel generator. Often the surgical team works on through the night.

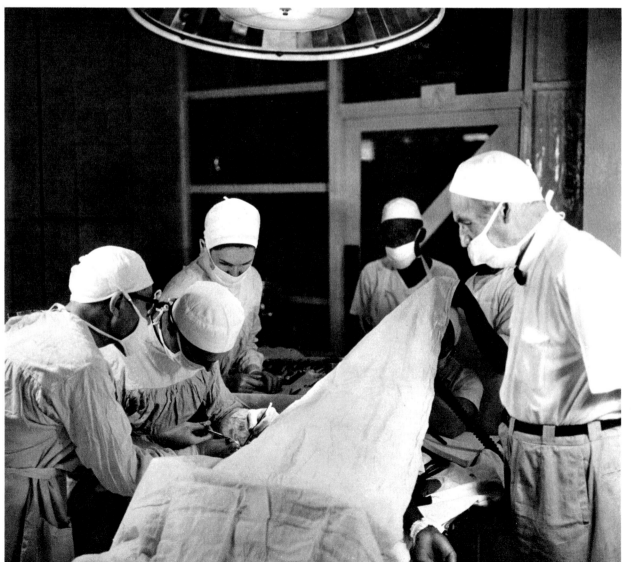

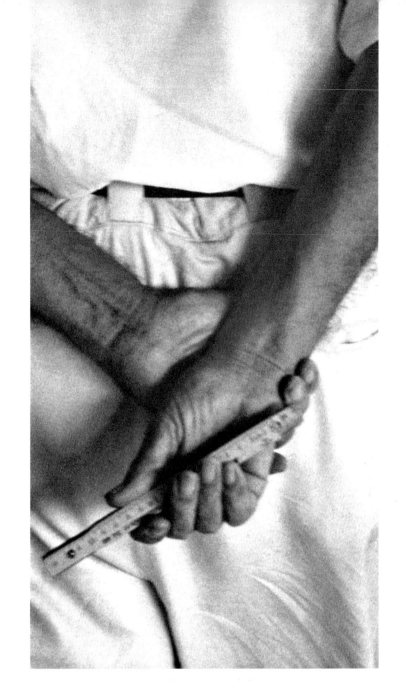

His hands express the variety of his many tasks.

TELEGRAM

I BEG THE FRENCH RADIO NETWORK [AT BRAZZAVILLE] NOT TO MAKE A SPECIAL OCCASION OF THE 14TH OF JANUARY AT LAMBARENE. I WISH TO CELEBRATE MY 80 YEARS IN SIMPLICITY AND TRANQUILITY WITH THE STAFF OF MY HOSPITAL.

DOCTOR SCHWEITZER

"I don't mind changes—but I want to know what they are." A. S.

Sitting on a pile of corrugated iron used for roofs, in the atelier or workshop, Schweitzer plans the next day's schedule

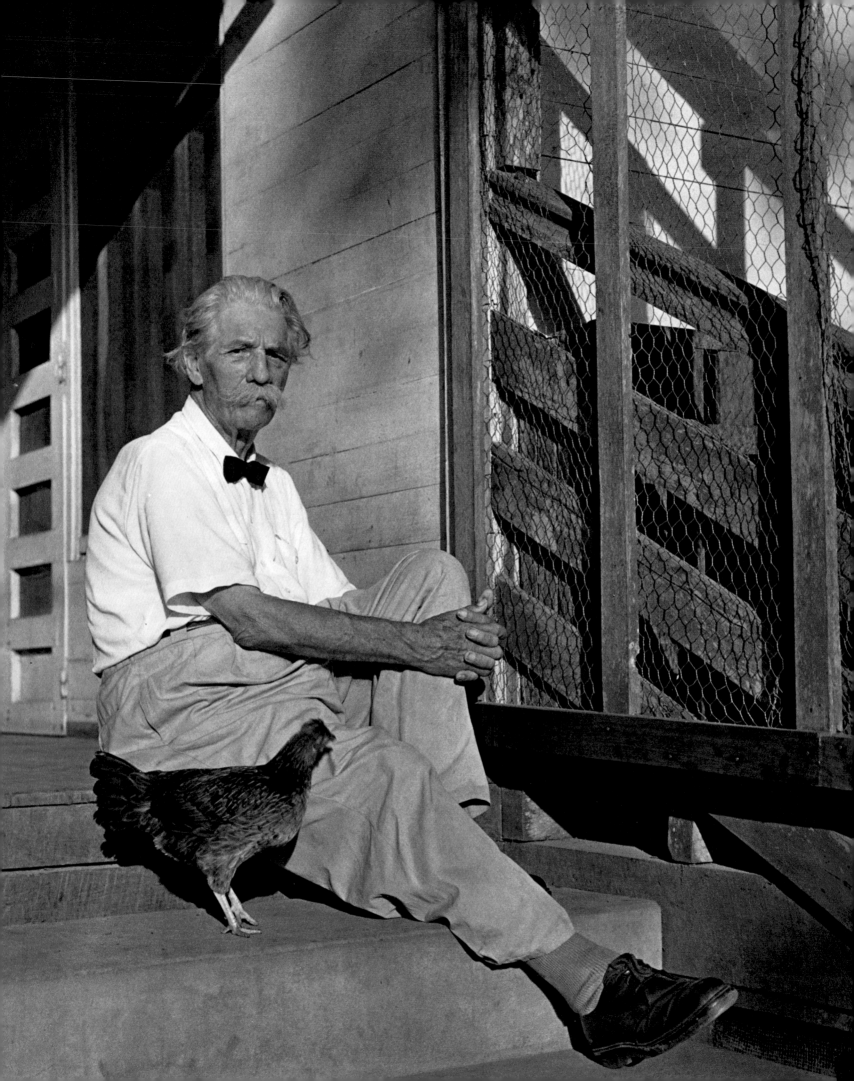

JOURNALIST: If you had to sum up your fifty years in Africa with a single event, with a tale, an anecdote, the most beautiful story, of these fifty years—?

A. S.: The most beautiful story of my fifty years here is that I have been able to help the sick . . . that is the most beautiful story.

1963

INTERVIEW WITH A JOURNALIST, 1963

Do you think that if you had spent these fifty years in France instead of Africa, your thought would have followed the same course?

A. S. The same, it would be the same.

You don't think you would have been influenced by the outside, and, well, by the pressure of civilization . . . ?

A. S. Civilization is morality . . . the true civilization is spiritual, isn't it?

But the modern world exerts a pressure for which you condemn it.

A. S. Pardon me?

The modern world exerts a pressure on the individual that you condemn.

A. S. I condemn it for not having respect for existence, the veneration of life.

So, in the context of a large city, you think you might have avoided these external pressures?

A. S. But I have lived in a large city. I lived for a fairly long time in Paris . . . and men are the same everywhere. I didn't feel pressures, no.

So, according to you, if, instead of having spent these fifty years here, you had spent them in Paris, you would still have arrived at the same conclusions today?

A. S. Oh! You mean a troubled world could disturb one's philosophical thought? Thought is always thought, it is born as thought, it remains thought.

Every evening after 5:30, when the last work bell had rung, Schweitzer and his pelican Parsifal would walk to the kitchen to get Parsifal's supper of fish. The bird was brought to the hospital because its wings had been clipped and it could not fish for itself. Parsifal guarded Schweitzer's room at night, pecking at intruders, until killed by a hunter off the hospital grounds.

Dear Sirs:

You have invited me to take part in this celebration so that I may personally receive the Peace Prize [at Munich] which you have had the kindness to grant me. How gladly would I have come! . . . But I am a man these days who cannot control his own time. I am in the midst of preparations for my early return to Africa, and it would be impossible for me to postpone it. I must arrange for purchases for my hospital and for packing and shipping supplies in time to leave with me on the boat for Africa. I don't know how I shall ever be able to do all that needs to be done; my capacity has now grown less; I feel a great weariness. . . .

Albert Schweitzer

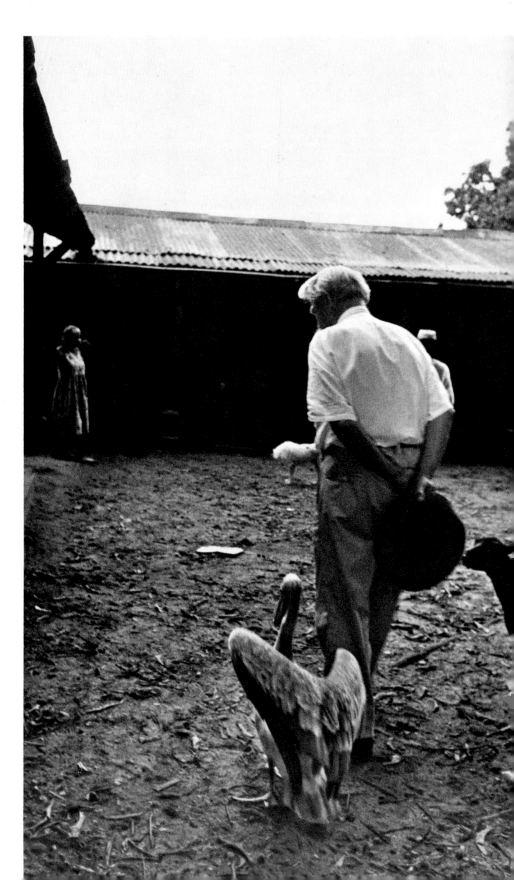

"The good man is the friend of all living things." A. S.

IV
THE COMMUNITY
OF
FRIENDSHIP

Friendship is a sharing of hope and anxiety and aspiration. For Schweitzer it is, even more, an expression of that reverence for life which acknowledges the sacredness of the individual personality.

For him, it is the direct personal encounter that is most real, and like his friend Martin Buber he sees in the confrontation of persons a practical philosophy. So important to him is the directness of encounter that he is uneasy with the telephone and telegraph because they seem to him a barrier separating man from man: "I cannot speak to someone I cannot see." Even in travel, he prefers a mode of transportation that makes it possible to meet people, but only late in life has he had the opportunity to travel by car—friends have offered to drive him in Europe from one engagement to another. On such trips he never fails to stop to pick up a hitchhiker or to offer a lift to burdened travelers. "One has a much more intimate relationship to the landscape and to people when one goes by car."

In conversation and even while lecturing he appears to concentrate upon one person in the group—a focusing of thought, not an exclusion of others. When one young man, hurt because Schweitzer looked elsewhere, said, "You never look at me," he answered: "But it isn't that I realize at whom I am looking. I am concentrating on trying to say as clearly as I can what I mean." A person who responds with eagerness to his conversation causes a reciprocal response: "I cannot talk unless I talk to *some*one and see the reaction in his face."

Everyone who is Schweitzer's friend—his neighbors in Günsbach, his patients in the Gabon, university professors, students, farmers, and royalty, all are to him of the same importance. He treats each with warmth. All persons are welcome at Lambarene; his hospitality is universal. When others criticize him for failing to discriminate among the persons to whom he gives his time and his energy, he pays no heed. A lonely and restless pilgrim may share as much of his time as a distinguished scientist. When his associates, fearful of the urgent and exhausting demands on his time, try zealously to protect him from the scores of visitors who come, he reprimands them: "Do not protect me." Even now, as a lesson to those who try to protect him, he tells how, thirty-five years ago in Sweden, he was resting at the home of a friend before giving an organ concert when someone he knew asked to see him but was turned away. He recalls how he looked for the man at the concert and, not seeing him, drove to his home but found he was not there. A letter of apology brought no answer. Schweitzer was deeply disturbed and promised himself never to disappoint anyone again.

Schweitzer respects others and accepts their ways; he allows the Gabonese to live at the hospital as they do in their native villages. Nor does he intrude in the personal affairs of others. With the shyness born of the awareness of another's right to independence and dignity, he asks no private questions. Nevertheless, it is apparent that his concern for others is profound. Anyone who seeks him out, stranger or friend, can find him. This compassionate concern makes people feel that he understands them, not as they seem to be, not as others judge them, but as they really are.

At night, after dinner, when the work day is done and he goes to his room, he says, "My door is open." Members of the staff come then with problems to be resolved; visitors come with questions, theological or personal. He is grateful when they show him the trust of their confidence. For many he is a brother, for many a father, for many a symbol of refuge.

In the world of living creatures, he rejects none. All animals, too, are included in his concept of friendship—he feels a deep responsibility toward them, as toward all living things, a responsibility precisely expressed in his philosophy of reverence for life.

Though he may sometimes feel critical, he tolerates mistakes and weaknesses others would condemn. He tries to teach through example and through understanding of the needs and difficulties of others. Loyalty is innate in his character, revealed in faithfulness to those who influenced his learning in his youth—mentors such as Goethe, Kant, and Bach—and in faithfulness to any person, young or old, who touches his life.

He is comfortable and relaxed with all kinds of people—earthy and warm with the peasants in Gunsbach, thoughtful and serious with scholars, practical with the laborers as they work together on the hospital construction. As soon as he has established contact—which does not take long—he uses with each person, instead of the formal "Sie," the German "du," which most of those who speak German consider appropriate only for close friends, children, or servants. He asks whether they would be willing to call him the same. Many hesitate in embarrassment because of his age and stature, and in a joking way he threatens to impose a fine for every "Sie." To those who feel his use of "du" to the natives implies more "servant" than "friend" he says simply: "When I pray to the good Lord, I say 'du.'"

Friendship is difficult to maintain when one person regards the other as a saint, and many consider Schweitzer a saint. He protests that he does not wish to be revered. "It is no basis for friendship," he says. And when a visitor greets him with, "What an honor to meet and to know you, Doctor," he responds, shaking hands vigorously: "What is honor? Say, instead, that you are pleased. No person is an honor to another."

Schweitzer is kind to people, but he is a human being. He is capable, for example, of outbursts of temper. But the natives are amused and even imitate him when he is angry. "Our dear old father has had a tantrum," they say. "How dare you laugh?" he protested one day, and a native answered, "You are Papa—can't an old Papa be angry?" He laughed then, too, for he cannot sustain his wrath for long. He is a man of many dimensions, a man who uses his senses fully, a man of feeling who is not afraid to express it. He accepts life with all its possibilities.

Letters are to Schweitzer an important link to people too distant for conversation. On all his travels he carries with him a white linen sack full of unanswered mail, hoping to find time to answer some. His largest personal expenditure is for stamps. In Africa more than a hundred letters a day pour in. Sometimes they have to wait for years before he can send a reply. All kinds of persons write to him—clergymen, gypsies, scholars, children, philosophers. The world may often seem far away in the jungle hospital, but it is, in letters, close at hand.

Many urge him to finish writing his books instead of devoting so much time to correspondence, but he continues to burrow through the stacks of letters even on Sunday when others rest. Asked to dictate or to use a typewriter, he refuses, believing he cannot establish contact with a person if a machine stands in the way. The people who write are as real to him as those he meets. Answering their letters is part of his philosophy of reverence for life, just like his availability at Lambarene to all who visit. If people come, must he not be there?

cop. 1

Rhena Eckert, Schweitzer's daughter, grew up in Europe. Now a laboratory technician and a mother, wife of Jean Eckert (left), a Zürich organ builder, she comes for part of each year to work in her father's hospital. Her oldest daughter Monique (second from right) has a boy of her own, the second daughter is studying to be a doctor, the third, Katherine (front), is gifted in music. The son, Philippe, is an organ builder like his father. This picture was taken in 1957.

Mme. Schweitzer and her husband in Lambarene with their dog Tschü Tschü (Choo Choo), one in a long line of dogs called "Choo Choo," for Rhena as a small child had called her dog by that name. This was Mme. Schweitzer's last sojourn in Africa—in 1957, a few months before her death.

Helene Bresslau Schweitzer, who trained as a nurse in order to help her husband, had suffered from the oppressive tropical climate. Schweitzer established a home for her in Königsfeld in the invigorating air of the Black Forest in a house given to him by the Brüdergemeinshaft, a religious group, but she was in ill health for many years. Even when in Europe she continued to help her husband, and in the 1930's she came to America to lecture for the hospital. After her death, Schweitzer returned the home to the group that had given it.

Schweitzer moves his belongings from Königsfeld to his Günsbach home after his wife's death: "Objects which Dr. Albert Schweitzer transported from his home on the Rue de Schramberg in Königsfeld . . . which he will no longer live in, to his home at Günsbach, Upper Rhine, on the road to Münster." Among the list of books (1,300), music notebooks, concert programs, paper, furniture (including the piano that "doesn't hold a tune any more"), valued from 1,000 to 30,000 francs, were these: "Manuscripts of Dr. A. Schweitzer, 12 packages—no value."

With Monique, his eldest granddaughter, at Güns-bach.

(Left to right) Schweitzer, his nephews Jean Jacques and Pierre Paul Schweitzer, with his brother Paul, a retired businessman, who lives across the street from his own home in Günsbach. Pierre Paul Schweitzer is director of the World Bank. Jean Jacques Schweitzer is an officer in the French Navy. There are many Schweitzers all over Europe. Whenever Schweitzer returned to the Continent he arranged a reunion, and sometimes more than a hundred came.

Katherine, Schweitzer's youngest granddaughter, at his piano in Günsbach.

The mother described in the letter lives on an island in the North Sea. She had rushed to Hamburg, learning Schweitzer was there, because she wanted him to baptize her children, but he was just leaving and invited her to Günsbach instead. He offered to write the following letter on learning the boy had been taken from school without permission.

Dear Dean:

I am appealing to you on behalf of the student K. E. His mother has made an effort to bring her two children to see me; I have been in contact with her for quite some time. She missed me when I was in Hamburg because she didn't know how short my stay there would be.

Now I learn from her that she has taken the boy to Günsbach without asking permission for him. As you may know, she is an unusual person, strange to the ways of the world. I beg of you not to make the child atone for the folly of his mother. It would pain me, since *I* would really be the cause of his being punished. I have scolded his mother. So for my sake I am asking that you punish him mildly and do not expel him from school. Do me, a tired old man, this favor, I beg of you: Be sure you have my deepest thanks.

> With best wishes,
> Your devoted,
> Albert Schweitzer

Children and young people are always in Schweitzer's life at the Lambarene hospital as well as in Europe. Every time he goes to Europe he accepts invitations to speak to school children, for he believes that the future of his philosophy lies with them.

Teachers from the nearby Protestant and Catholic mission schools at Lambarene come often to confer with Schweitzer about the progress, or lack of it, of the children who live in the hospital village. For children in the leper village, school is conducted regularly.

Schweitzer's sense of humor emerges often in playful ways. He wrote to Penelope, Dr. Emeric Percy's gorilla, this letter clearly intended for Dr. Percy himself. The reference to the electric bulbs is a teasing comment from Schweitzer because Dr. Percy was the first to rig a line for light into his quarters —he needed it for midnight medical study.

Günsbach August 22, 1955

Mlle. Penelope
c/o Dr. Percy
Lambarene Hospital

Dear Penelope:

These lines should tell you that I think of you affectionately as always and am homesick for you. Here in Europe I see nothing to compare to you—to the sweetness of your expression. Be good, and stay well. By the way: tell Dr. Percy, at some moment when he is in a good mood, that I would appreciate it very much if every two weeks he sent me a short report about everything he has to tell me about himself, the personnel, the hospital activities, the work, and the functioning of the motors. I know that if you are the spokesman, he cannot help doing as you wish. Who could resist you? But don't scold him for not having done it up till now. Such criticism coming from you might hurt him too much. Rest well on the news-papers, in the glowing light of the electric bulbs.

From the heart, yours
Albert Schweitzer

Dr. Rolf Müller, a young Swiss, was chief surgeon. He came in answer to an advertisement in a Zürich newspaper several years ago, during an emergency when—by contrast with the usual situation of a list of volunteers too long to accommodate—the hospital was suddenly without a surgeon. In the first four years of his stay he took no vacation.

Schweitzer with Dr. Larimer Mellon, director of the Albert Schweitzer hospital in Haiti. Dr. Mellon became a doctor in response to Schweitzer's influence. There are now six hospitals named for him, Dr. Mellon's; Dr. Theodore Binder's in Purcallpa, Peru; Dr. E. Gaine Cannon's in Balsam Grove, North Carolina; Dr. Humberto Sa's in Guarapuana, Brazil; Dr. Timothy Rhe's on an island off Korea; another in Basutoland in southern Africa.

Dr. Fergus Pope, who has been in training abroad to serve on the hospital staff, with Schweitzer in Günsbach. He had come to Lambarene on a world tour, but after a two-month stay told Schweitzer he had decided to become a doctor and to return to serve the sick of the Gabon.

In London in 1955 Schweitzer set up headquarters in Emil Mettler's little tearoom just off the Strand. He had come to England to receive the Order of Merit from the Queen, with General Eisenhower hitherto the only non-Briton to win the honor. Bertrand Russell (above, left) came to see him there to discuss the threat of nuclear warfare. So did Vaughan Williams (above, right), chiefly to talk about music—and, naturally, Bach.

Fritz Behn with Schweitzer in Günsbach. Behn had come to model Schweitzer for a sculpture.

With Jean Rostand, the noted French biologist and author, in Rostand's villa outside Paris in 1957.

Schweitzer with his friend, Nikos Ka-zantzakis, distinguished Greek writer, who died in 1957.

At Lambarene mail goes into a big wicker basket. Mlle. Mathilda Kottmann answers many letters for him in Lambarene, Mme. Emmy Martin in Günsbach. Schweitzer used to try always to add a personal touch to each letter, addressing it himself, adding a message at the end. A letter is never closed until the last minute in case he has time to add a postscript. Schweitzer will not abbreviate dates in his letters (as, 14.3.65) because he thinks it a sign of haste and therefore impolite.

"If my correspondence were to be published one day, it would make twenty-five volumes!"   A. S.

"Among friends, when someone is angry at you, always leave the door open for reconciliation."   A. S.

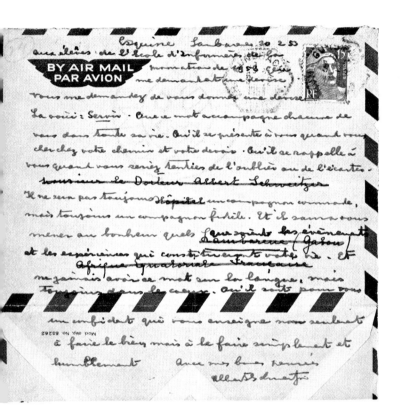

Schweitzer writes the first drafts of many of his letters on the backs of old envelopes to save paper. His correspondence reflects his many concerns, in recent years especially the nuclear arms race and the threat to peace.

. . . Once again we are in danger of succumbing to inhumanity. Few governments take seriously the horrible effects of atomic explosions and even of test explosions and many are inclined to go along with this inhumanity. That is why I have entered the struggle against nuclear weapons, although I am almost too old to take part. But I can still accomplish something—since as a recipient of the Nobel Peace Prize I have the privilege of speaking in full freedom over Radio Oslo on all matters concerning peace, including the danger of nuclear weapons to the world.

The main point I use as an argument against nuclear weapons is that they are against international law. This argument is irrefutable. International law permits only weapons that can be aimed at a specific, limited target, so that no nonparticipants outside the scope of these weapons are affected. Even in atomic tests, radioactive fallout is dispersed over great distances, causing terrible ravages. Just imagine what would happen in the event of an atomic war!

But international law has expressly framed laws for mankind regarding the use of weapons—laws which forbid the use and practice of atomic and thermonuclear weapons. It is incomprehensible that jurists should not have raised their voices as soon as atomic and hydrogen weapons appeared on the scene and pointed out that they were contrary to international law. In all negotiations up till now this point has remained outside the discussion. But this argument must play its proper role in the fight against these weapons. Only then will we succeed in banning nuclear weapons and thus safeguard ourselves from the dangers of atomic war. . . .

Albert Schweitzer

Schweitzer and Louis Meyer at Günsbach. A portrait in oils of the young Schweitzer hangs above the piano.

Some years ago Louis Meyer, a New York sculptor, bought a ticket to Günsbach in the hopes of sculpting Schweitzer's hands. He presented himself at Schweitzer's door, the fortieth visitor of the day, and members of the household turned him away. He stopped in the Günsbach church to brood over his misfortune. Schweitzer, who came to practice the organ that afternoon, found the dejected stranger and asked what was troubling him. Distressed at the story, Schweitzer invited him to stay at his home. When the sculptured hands were exhibited, a woman admired them and wrote to Meyer; then began a friendship by mail that became love. Schweitzer married them in a village church near the Rhine. Louis Meyer was eighty-eight, his bride in her sixties.

Schweitzer and Father Dominique Pire of Belgium, another holder of the Nobel Prize for Peace, also in Günsbach. Father Pire has named a village for European refugees after Schweitzer.

After a visit to the mayor of Tübingen, West Germany, Schweitzer steps out on a balcony to respond to the crowd that has gathered to greet him. He had been invited to Tübingen to receive an honorary degree of law from the University.

A Norwegian girl asks for and gets her autograph, outside the Nobel Institute in Oslo, 1954.

The young philosophy student whom Schweitzer advised to help build a road as preparation for hard thought.

Madame Schweitzer

With a child prodigy at the Strasbourg organ of St. Thomas's. The boy's father had wanted Schweitzer's opinion.

"Think how difficult life must be for royalty!" A. S.

Schweitzer and Queen Elisabeth of the Belgians, one of his oldest friends, herself in her eighties, at the Günsbach organ. She tried to come to Günsbach every time he visited Europe. They took long walks together, and he played the organ for her every afternoon as villagers gathered in the church.

Maman Sans-Nom, a pigmy, wandered into the hospital many years ago speaking a jumbled dialect no one has ever been able to understand. She adopted the hospital as her home and has lived a primitive life of her own in a roofed-in open space between two buildings. She refuses to live in a room. Next door is the mortuary. She cries for every death and holds a wake with every bereaved family.

Schweitzer and Pablo Casals, famed cellist, are united in friendship by their love of music and of humanity. One of their rare meetings occurred in Zürich after a concert by Casals.

Schweitzer in Günsbach with a village friend.

Augustus John, great Welsh portrait painter, asked the art critic of the Sunday Times, *John Russell, to stay with him all night to be sure he remained sober and woke in time for a sitting with Schweitzer in the morning. The painter made this drawing that morning in London.*

Schweitzer in Paris on his daily walk to a favorite bistro, Le Voltaire, with his old friend and associate Mme. Emmy Martin.

Schweitzer goes out of his way to visit a remote Swiss Alpine village to thank an old woman who, for scores of years, sent all the egg money from her small farmyard to the Lambarene hospital.

Schweitzer with some of his school classmates, at a reunion in Günsbach.

"My philosophy has come from thought." A. S.

V
THE UNITY OF THOUGHT

The purpose of philosophy is the search for truth, and for Schweitzer this search can be undertaken only in spiritual freedom and in devotion to reason. Religious truth deserves man's highest and best thought. Thought and inquiry lead to effective deed: "The most important thing in education is to make young people think for themselves."

Man's life should be consistent in feeling, belief, and action; no part should war against another. Schweitzer has tried to order his own life to this end, dedicating himself to the philosophy that seems to him true in mind and body and spirit. In his healing ministry, he works to save life; in his ministry of music, he affirms the harmony of thought and the splendor of human aspiration; in his thought he reflects and writes, that his ideas may reach beyond the boundaries of his hospital and beyond the limits of his own life. Schweitzer believes that if a philosophy is true and good, it ought to be tested in the world. "Reality never submits to theory." "The trouble with philosophers is that they stay in their chair instead of voicing their opinions and trying to influence the leaders of politics."

Whenever an hour can be found after the busy rounds of the day, he sits at his table writing in his firm neat hand with his old-fashioned pen. The kerosene lamp casts a soft light over the white room with its white cotton cloth on the table, the white cotton curtains at the windows. Many books have been published since the first, written in his student days, but in recent years he has given his strength to the hospital, finding time to work only intermittently on the third volume of his *Philosophy of Civilization*. But his work on a study of the Kingdom of God continues. The completed manuscript piles up on shelves or hangs in batches from nails above his table. The work proceeds slowly, interrupted constantly by a demanding correspondence and the burdens of a hospital community. There is no real privacy, no rest: "Some of my thoughts I had to carry for years in my head before I found the time to put them on paper."

He will not publish a manuscript until he has made many revisions, just as, years ago, he did not deliver a sermon until several drafts had been made, perfecting the precision of his expression, deepening the thrust of his thought. "We have to dig into depth; that is what counts. It is not the height of a drilling machine that is important, only how deep it can drill." As he walked in his plantation of fruit trees one day, he said, "Roots standing in good soil, in soil well looked after, have always seemed to me the symbol of a healthy mind. No tree of the mind can grow and develop when the fundamental ethical principle is not deeply rooted."

To Schweitzer reason and emotion are—or ought to be—reconciled to each other. He is a man of thought, but of emotion besides: "I am not ashamed to be sentimental—with respect to either my ideals or my feelings." His love of music is in part a commitment of intellect, but in part the response of an artist to whom beauty brings exaltation and serenity of spirit. If a man's feeling and a man's reflection serve the same end, he is at one with himself; the conflict within his mind and heart yields to peace.

And though he believes that thought, to be healthy, must be deeply rooted and carefully tended, and though his own thought is profound, he feels that it is, essentially, simple and easily understood: "I am a childlike philosopher." To revere life and to serve it because all life is one, this is the heart of his commitment and his faith.

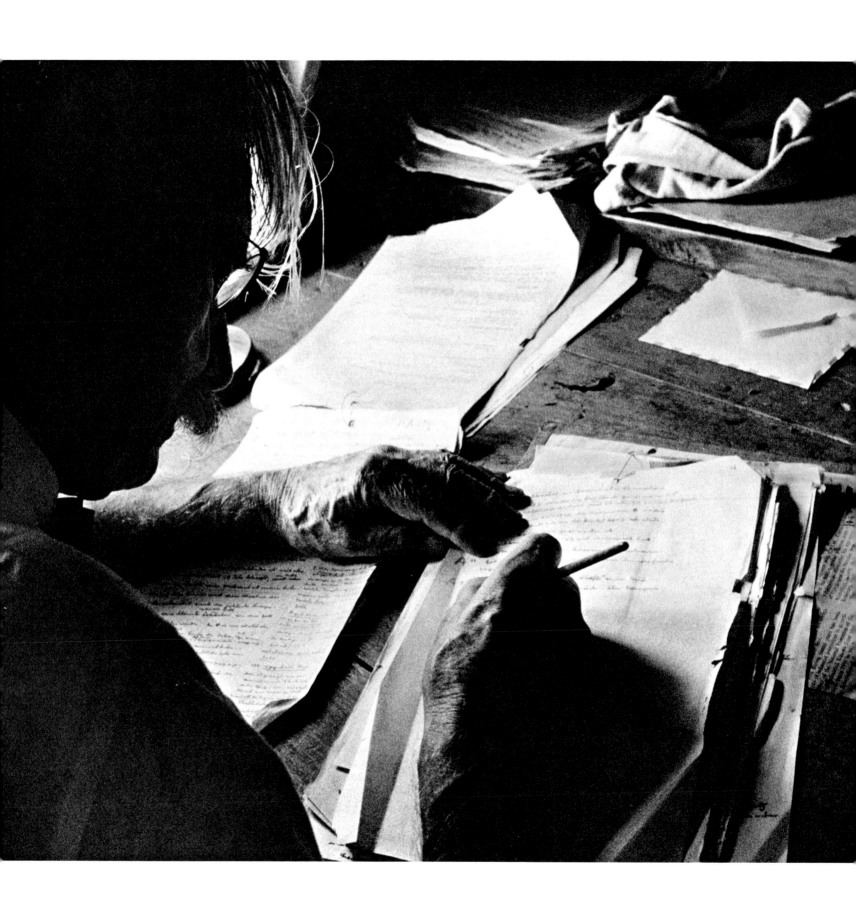

Lambarene, Febr. 13, 1953

Dear Friend:

I do not want to miss joining those who wish you well on your 70th birthday. In view of the work you still have to offer, I would wish it were the 50th, but since it is after all the 70th, let us all be happy that you are still so wonderfully strong and wish that you may stay that way for a long time to come.

If in the future someone writes the history of the German publishing houses in the 20th century, he will have to report that extraordinary events endangered their existence in the first half of the century. But at the same time, he can declare that they did not lose courage despite their distress, but generated the energy to survive and to achieve astonishing feats.

Among the names of those hardest hit and the most courageous and determined yours, dear friend, will rank very high. What you accomplished is unbelievable to us who witnessed it. We know also what spirit gave you the strength to start again from scratch in spite of two total collapses occasioned by those terrible events. That spirit was the high esteem in which you held your profession. You wished once again to provide for today's generation books of worth, so that, as in the past, they could partake of the cultural and spiritual values books transmit. Many of today's young people will be as grateful to you as we of the older generation were when with your Philosophical Library you gave them the chance to learn the works of great thinkers unknown until then. I myself was deeply grateful to you even before our personal acquaintance. When I mention the importance of your Philosophical Library, I am fully aware that I express the thoughts of many of the past generation; and they still think so. We are glad that through your activity the present generation will have the same privilege we had.

May I add a note of strictly personal thanks: if you had not forced me to write *Aus meinem Leben und Denken* (*Out of My Life and Thought*) I never would have thought of it. You used a publisher's diplomacy when I was busy with quite different tasks, and in 1929 you persuaded me to write my autobiography for you for *Philosophie der Gegenwart in Selbstdarstellungen* (*Philosophy of the Present*).

If you, dear friend, had not enjoyed Oskar Kraus's co-operation, I doubt whether you would have succeeded. I did not like the whole thing, because at the age of 54 years I believed I was still too young to write a report of my life. An old clergyman in Strasbourg had stopped me in the street: "What have I been told, Albert, that you are writing your life already? That is a symptom of vanity. A man should do that only after his 70th birthday. I want to hear this from me. Don't be offended." He spoke these words and left me. I did not think he was wrong, but it so happened that Mr. Felix Meiner thought differently. And after he received the short autobiography, it was almost inevitable that by itself it grew into *Aus meinem Leben und Denken*.

Without your stubbornness as a publisher, dear friend, I would not have written that document about the essence and thinking of a period now far gone. For at 70 I would not have been able to write these memoirs. The circumstances of 1945 and the following years did not permit contemplative absorption in the past, not to mention the fact that I would not have had enough time at my disposal to write.

Now, no more words about the publisher. In the quietness of the tropical night allow me, dear friend, to tell you that I liked you also as a human being right from the first time I met you, and that our close, cordial friendship over these long years means much to me. I am looking forward to the day when I shall see you again in Hamburg and plan to have ample time for you when we meet.

Tomorrow morning a native will take this letter in a canoe downstream to the post office in Lambarene. In the afternoon it will fly over my hospital in a plane and will continue its flight over the branches of the palm trees on its way north.

With cordial greetings,
Yours very sincerely,
Albert Schweitzer

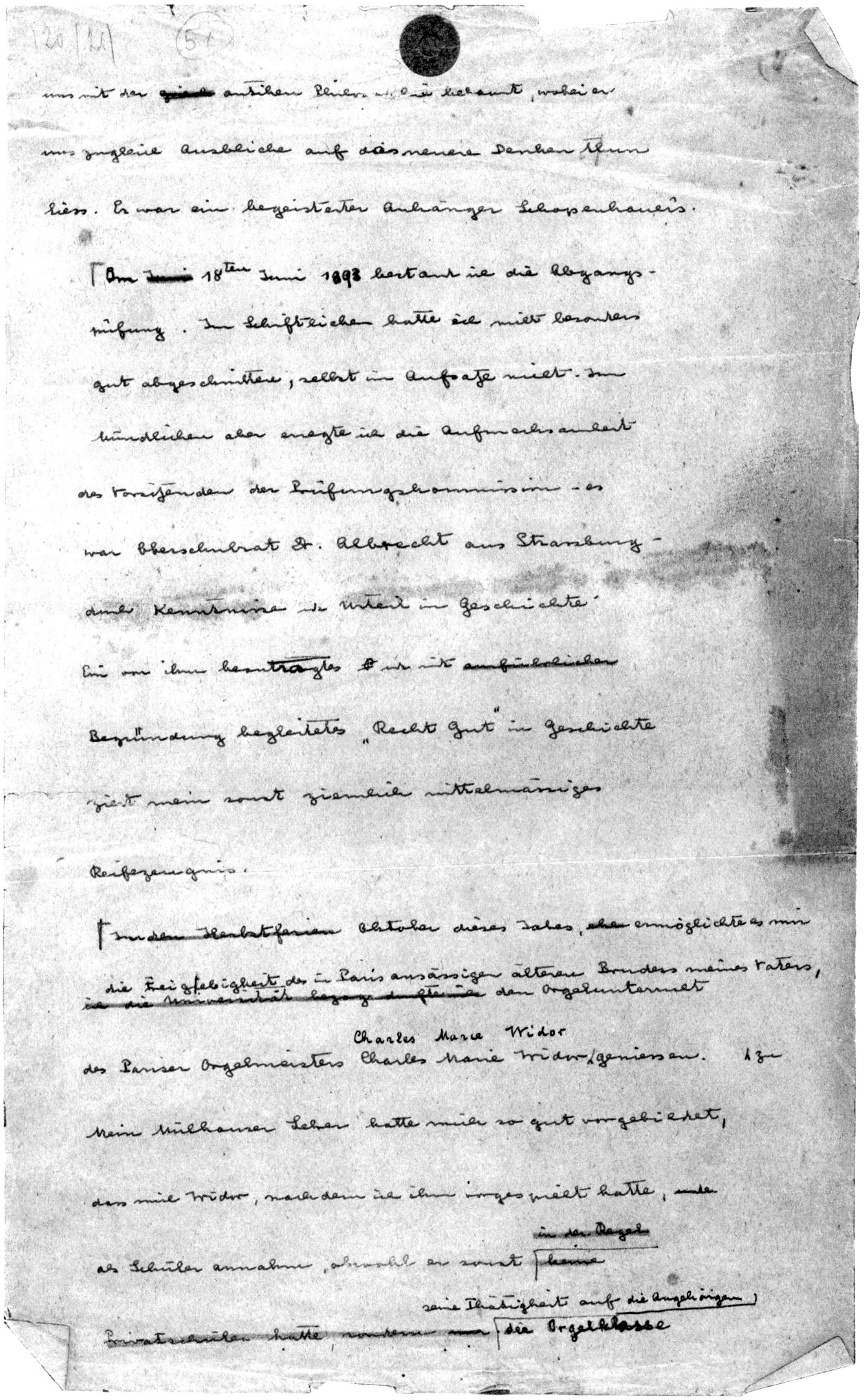

On this veranda at the mission station where he first started his hospital, Schweitzer in 1915 began the writing of his *Philosophy of Civilization*.

At Port Gentil, Schweitzer always spends the night at the Protestant mission before sailing for Europe and on his return to his hospital in Lambarene. Even on these short stops he tries to answer correspondence.

He writes whenever and wherever he can, in hotels, railroad stations, automobiles, restaurants. He completed his book *The Mysticism of Paul the Apostle* on board ship in 1929.

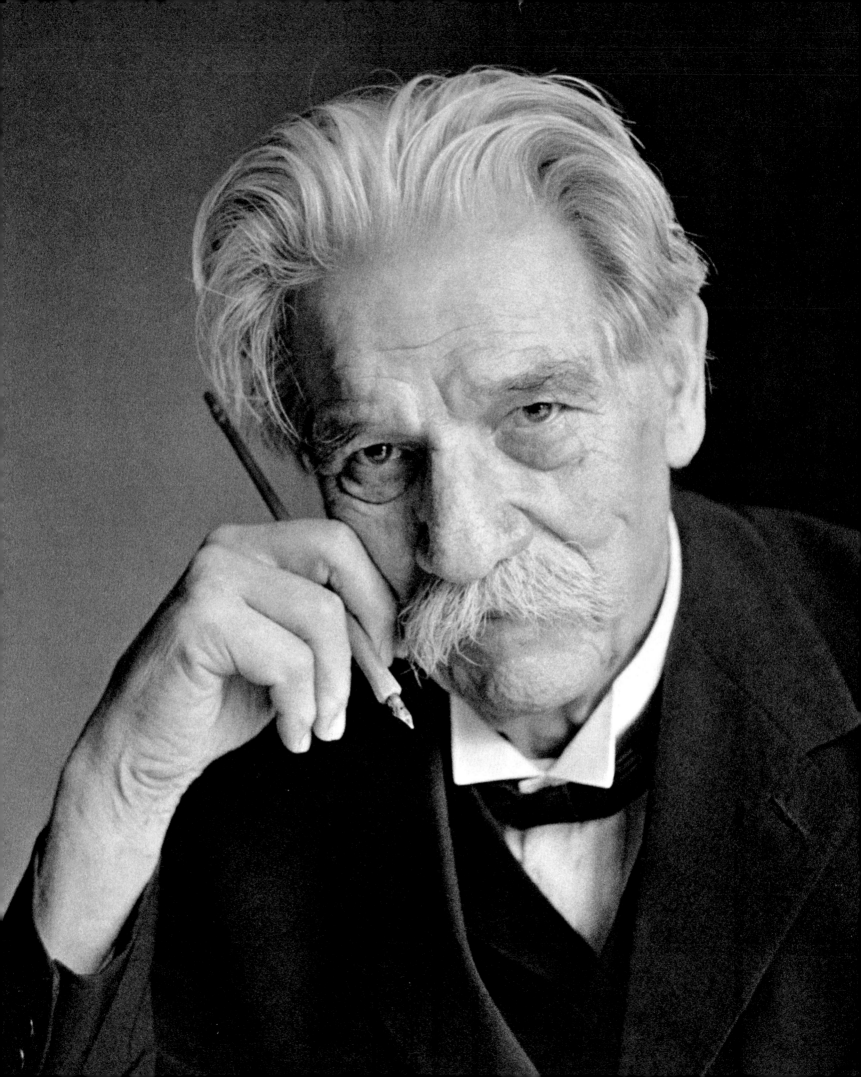

CONVERSATION WITH A JOURNALIST, 1963

I've read in one of your works that you were very much moved at the sight of a microbe under a microscope, and that you said to yourself that you were about to destroy a human life.

A. S.   No, not a "human life," a *life,* a life. . . .

My mistake . . . a life that you were about to destroy . . . how do you reconcile that with the demands of science?

A. S.   Necessity forces us to sacrifice lives. You tread on them. You crush ants. . . . *But:* we must try as much as possible to respect all life. That is our constant battle.

So, there's a problem of selection.

A. S.   Oh, far from that. I don't know of any "problems of selection."

But in so far as you choose between lives . . . in so far as you choose between lives, there are lives that you save at the expense of others.

A. S.   One must save every life when one can. And necessity *obliges* us to sacrifice. And it's most painful to sacrifice. . . .

But isn't there a limit, or should one save even the lives of microbes and parasites?

A. S.   Well, I respect them.

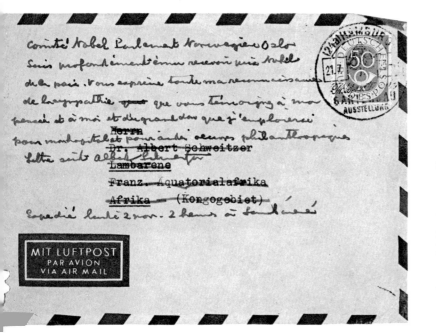

TO THE NOBEL COMMITTEE, NORWEGIAN PARLIAMENT, OSLO

I am deeply moved to receive the Nobel Peace Prize. I wish to express all my gratitude for the understanding you manifest for my thought and for me, and for the large gift, which I will plan to use for my hospital and for philanthropic work. (*Letter mailed by Albert Schweitzer, Monday, November 2 at 2 o'clock from Lambarene*)

TO THE NOBEL PRIZE COMMITTEE AT OSLO

I wish to say to His Majesty, King Haakon, to you who are members of the Committee, and to all those who join you on December 10, how much I regret not being able to come to Oslo for the presentation of the prize. For many reasons, I cannot leave my hospital at this time for the voyage to Oslo. I will be with you in thought on December 10. Let me tell you how I have been impressed by the honor that has been given to me and by the sympathy shown to me. I believe that I'm not mistaken in supposing that it is the ideas I have expressed which have won for me the attention of those who awarded the prize. To receive it is an encouragement to continue. It is also a precious aid to construct a village to house the 250 lepers cared for at my hospital. It will pay for cement, lumber, and necessary linens, for to minister to a good end is work. I would be delighted to come to Oslo next year during a visit I wish to make to Europe. For many years I have wished to come, but haven't found the time. Now I have a reason which impels me to come. I am deeply happy about it.

Albert Schweitzer

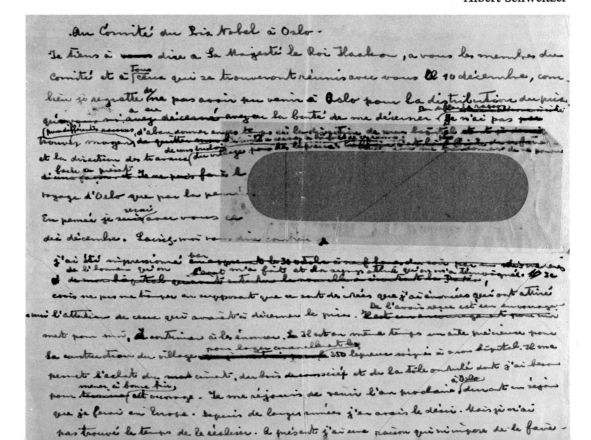

A rough outline written, as noted by Schweitzer in the upper left hand corner, "In the night of October 4–5, 1954." These are the original notes for his Oslo speech on acceptance of the Nobel Prize for Peace.

A HUMANITY OF CULTURE (FROM A SPEECH TO SCHOOL CHILDREN)

"Then I asked myself: how can we spread among men what we so sorely need in our present predicament, so that we shall again become what we once wanted to be—a humanity of culture?

"And living in a remote place, I imagined to myself the fate of the nations now rising out of dependence into independence who must also develop themselves spiritually, and I asked myself: how then will these nations attain culture, when *we* live a cultureless life? Again and again I said to myself: they must *get* something from us, for we do have a great cultural past which cannot be extinguished. . . . We of the old world have to help all the nations in this new world. We must bring life to them—and not always merely take from them.

"Then I asked myself: how can this ethic prevail in the world and become the basis for a world philosophy?

"The answer came from a German school.

"A few teachers asked me if they could name their school the Albert Schweitzer School. Well, why not, I thought, if it gives them pleasure. Then I thanked the school and wrote: May all your students, as they think back on their school in later years, feel gratitude toward their teachers, as I have felt gratitude throughout my life toward my teachers in the *Gymnasium* at Mülhouse for everything I received from them. May those who have been privileged to study in this school not only acquire knowledge but also, as they develop into adults, become true educators. Well, that is what I wrote. Soon there was another school, then three, five, seven—and I always wrote the same thing. Until suddenly I said to myself: That is the way! The school will be the way! From the time they start school, young people must be imbued with the idea of reverence for all living things. Then we will be able to develop a spirit based on ethical responsibility and one that will stir many. Then we will be entitled to call ourselves a humanity of culture." A. S.
Hamburg, 1959

Schweitzer perusing the revision of the French translation of his autobiography with Professor Robert Minder of the Sorbonne, in the Hotel Paris-Dinard, 1959.

The notes of which a fragment is reproduced here were written by Schweitzer in an automobile on his way to Brussels in November 1959, to deliver a speech. The original manuscript was lost when Schweitzer asked if the car could stop to pick up a hitchhiker and the manuscript fell out in a bundle by the roadside. A vain search was made back over the road. Everyone but Schweitzer was upset. He said only, "Don't worry. I have it all in my head." These notes were the substitute.

A fragment of Schweitzer's notes for a speech in Paris, November 11, 1959, written in a car. A bumpy road caused the change to almost indecipherable script.

Because of persistent writer's cramp, Schweitzer finds it easier to write with his pen held between his second and third fingers. Here are samples of his handwriting as he tests several new pens.

Ich glaube, dass ich mit
dieser Feder schreiben kann

Sie ist nicht ganz gut.

Jetzt soll ich noch

Es geht gut mit dieser Feder.

Das ist
Dies ist eine guter Feder
Es ist wirklich eine Freude
damit zu schreiben.

Schweitzer's desk at Günsbach

"Thought is the strongest thing we have. Work is done by true and profound thought. That is a real force." A. S.

A page showing Schweitzer's method of preparing a manuscript. First, he prepares a detailed outline at the side in a narrow column. Then he develops his thought on the rest of the page, writing in small firm script, revising as he goes.

ALBERT SCHWEITZER IN AN INTERVIEW OVER RADIO BRAZZAVILLE, 1953

"I was always, even as a boy, engrossed in the philosophical problem of the relation between emotion and reason. Certain truths originate in feeling, others in the mind. Those truths that we derive from our emotions are of a moral kind—compassion, kindness, forgiveness, love for our neighbor. Reason, on the other hand, teaches us the truths that come from reflection.

"But with the great spirits of our world—the Hebrew prophets, Christ, Zoroaster, the Buddha, and others—feeling is always paramount. In them emotion holds its ground against reason, and all of us have an inner assurance that the truth of emotion that these great spiritual figures reveal to us is the most profound and the most important truth.

"The problem presented itself to me in these terms: must we really be condemned to live in this dualism of emotional and rational truths? Since my particular preoccupation was with problems of morality, I have always been struck by finding myself forced to recognize that the morality elaborated by philosophy, both ancient and modern, has been meager indeed when compared to the morality of the great religions and ethical geniuses who have taught us that the supreme and only truth capable of satisfying man's spirit is love.

"I reached a point where I asked myself this question: does the mind, in its striving for a morality that can guide us in life, lag so far behind the morality that emotion reveals because it is not sufficiently profound to be able to conceive what the great teachers, in obedience to feeling, have made known to us?

"This led me to devote myself entirely to the search for a fundamental principle of morality. Others before me have done the same. Throughout history there have been philosophers who believed intuitively that reason must eventually succeed in discovering the true and profound nature of the good. I have tried to carry their work further. In so doing, I was brought to the point where I had to consider the question of what the fundamental idea of existence is. What is the mind's point of departure when it sets itself to the task of reflecting on humanity and on the world in which we live? This point of departure, I said to myself, is not any knowledge of the world that we have acquired. We do not have—and we will never have—true knowledge of the world; such knowledge will always remain a mystery to us.

"The point of departure naturally offered for meditation between ourselves and the world is the simple evidence that we are life that wishes to live and are animated by a will to live in the midst of other lives animated by the same will. Simply by considering the act of thinking, our consciousness tells us this. True knowledge of the world consists in our being penetrated by a sense of the mystery of existence and of life.

"If we proceed on the basis of this knowledge, it is no longer isolated reason that devotes itself to thought, but our whole being, that unity of emotion and reflection that constitutes the individual.

tening to the sound of the organ at St. Thomas's Church, Strasbourg

"If I am penetrated by this knowledge of the mysterious value of all life, I am then able to understand what my attitude should be toward the world around me, which is composed of other lives. We have the obligation to respect all will-to-life as if it were our own. We are endowed with the faculty of sharing the lives of other beings, in their joys and fears and grief. This characteristic—I would even say this perfection—which the Scottish philosopher Hume was the first to advance philosophically in the second half of the eighteenth century, dictates our behavior in life. It reveals the fundamental idea of the good, which is that the good consists in preserving life, in supporting it, in seeking to carry it to its highest value. Evil consists in destroying life, in injuring it, or in thwarting its full flowering.

"The weak point of morality until now has been its too-narrow basis. Morality was concerned only with our behavior toward other men. It was a tree the roots of which were not deeply or widely enough spread to grow as they should. It did not live; it vegetated.

"Morality progresses from being specific to being universal. It must make this advance. The idea of the good can take complete possession of us only if it is fully recognized, and if we widen our responsibility toward men to include all creatures. It has been held that to do this was a sentimental impulse going beyond the borders of ordinary morality—a kind of unnecessary supplement. The belief has been held that cruelty toward animals could exist side by side with the concept of the good without impairing it. The claim is still made that it is perfectly proper to inflict pain and suffering on human beings in order to amuse them (as in bullfights, those hideous spectacles are defended today in our country where they were once unknown). The concept of respect for life constitutes a deepening and a quickening of morality which helps us to achieve a spiritual progress—a progress for which the hour has struck and of which both individuals and nations stand in great need.

"When man sets himself, as a unity of reason and emotion, to meditating and to reasoning, emotion and reason are in accord. The principle of respect for life is the same as the principle of love of the great moral and religious spirits. It states and defines in philosophical, reasoned language what has been revealed to these noble elect. Every human being who has the courage to allow his mind to probe deeply into the nature of truth will discover in himself the idea of that love which is supreme knowledge—the light that will illumine his path through life. The idea carries implicit difficulties, since all of us may find ourselves faced with the unavoidable necessity of causing other creatures suffering and even death. These problems can worry and upset us, but they cannot shake our conviction that we must be guided by respect for life and that we must practice it wherever and whenever possible, in order to remain in harmony with all that is best in us."

Listening to the organ played by Marcel Dupres before church services, St. Sulpice, Paris

Sweden

THORNTON WILDER: "Tell me, Doctor, at the age you have reached, how do you feel about the loves of your youth—Bach, Wagner, Goethe, Kant, Hegel? One does change in the course of a lifetime."

ALBERT SCHWEITZER: "Moi? Je suis fidel." (Me? I am faithful.)

At a Paris restaurant, 1953

This piano, zinc-lined against the jungle climate and with organ pedal attachments, was sent to Schweitzer by the Paris Bach Society. Often, at night, he played Bach here. He shipped it back to Günsbach in 1961 because there was less and less time to play.

Schweitzer's notes for an organ concert program.

Studying a Bach score, in 1959 at Tübingen, where Bach manuscripts were stored during World War II.

What is the purpose of life for both mankind and the individual?

What general belief or philosophy would you suggest as a guide for the younger generation regardless of political belief, religion, or class?

How can your philosophy be understood and applied by the modern city man at his work and at his often boring routine of everyday life?

How can man become inspired or find the drive necessary to work to the extent of his abilities, not only in his contacts with life and the living, but also in providing the material necessities for himself and society?

DR. SCHWEITZER'S ANSWERS

One cannot explain life. Everything is a mystery to us. All we know is that there is one thing—to be alive. And another state: not being alive. It took aeons for life to evolve. We don't know how life arose out of chemical materials, nor do we know how many years it took to change dead matter into life. Neither do we know the "goal" of mankind, where it is heading. All we do know is that life is a great mystery and that we ought to be filled with awe and reverence for this mystery.

We must explain to ourselves and understand that everything that lives is related to us. Our respect must reach all that is alive. We must not hurt another life. We should kill only under compulsion of absolute necessity. Each wounding or killing is a guilt we impose upon ourselves. We must help. This is our responsibility. We must move into a true and deep relationship with other beings. To live in true humanity means to be inspired by the idea of reverence for all life. A factory worker who sees a fly on his machine will hit and kill it if he has not become aware of the wonder of life. But once he knows, he will not kill it thoughtlessly, but help to free it if he sees it caught in a room. He will open the window and let it go. If he finds a creature that needs help (and everyone finds such creatures), he will help. This will bring him happiness because he realizes that it is in his power to act for good.

We people have invented many things, but we have not mastered the creation of life. We cannot even create an insect. Therefore, though freeing a fly may seem insignificant, it should remind man of the mystery of life, and the respect he should have for such life—should make him a more human, thinking being.

Everyone must work to live, but the purpose of life is to serve and to show compassion and the will to help others. Only then have we ourselves become true human beings.
Copenhagen, 1959

AFTER A TALK AT A FACTORY IN PARIS IN 1959, SCHWEITZER ANSWERED QUESTIONS FROM THE AUDIENCE

QUESTION *Do you not think that a profound disequilibrium exists between science, the progress which strides on like a giant, and man, whose progress toward moral understanding proceeds at the pace of a tortoise?*

A. S. Nonsense, science pursues its own way, and we cannot stop it. It has given us immense benefits; it has put us into great danger. But we can escape this danger if we find men capable of surmounting all the circumstances of life and the difficulties of our time. It is only through the spirit that we can conquer. And I admit to you, I believe in man. My long life has convinced me that we are all thinking beings, and the question is only whether thought does dare us to reach to the depth of our being. There we will find that we are entirely different from what we are when we do not search our own depths. All thinking being comes to the knowledge that thought is the road which leads toward higher ethics of the spirit. It is my faith. It is that which sustains me in my life.

QUESTION *Do you think that life's heavy demands upon individuals have no influence on their behavior as men?*

A. S. I believe that all of us have something in us that illumines our own vision and our understanding of others, and that we are all a candle for others. It has been my experience that one small act can take possession of us suddenly to move and lead us.

QUESTION *How is it, amid all the suffering of men on the earth and all the suffering of animals on the earth—for instance, in laboratory experiments—that there is the useful pain which causes good, and useless pain which leads to nothing?*

A. S. Monsieur, do not ask me to discuss now the great problem of experiments on animals. I am not prepared, and it is a difficult question. Most important of all, and this is what we judge as progress, is that those who perform them should be aware of the terrible responsibility of their experiments. And we all, when we see suffering, must be challenged by a desire for redemption, to help all creatures. There is always mystery, we move within the mist of a great mystery: the mystery of pain. And we come to be always conscious of our great responsibility to alleviate it.

Now, since there are no more questions, permit me to ask one myself. I forgot, in my talk, to state precisely that morality does not begin with man but is already present in many creatures. The great progress in the evolution of life is that a moment arrives when we see what lies around us, comprehend what is, and accept our place in it. It is the last great step in the spiritual existence of each of us and of humanity, to come to the point where one does not live ones life for oneself alone, but lives with others, to live the life of others within their life. This is the final accomplishment, the final progress which a living thing makes, and every creature already has in itself the beginning of this participation in the life of others.

"We are like waves that do not move individually but rise and fall in rhythm. To share, to rise and fall in rhythm with life around us, is a spiritual necessity." A. S., *"Paris Notes"*

TWO KINDS OF DISCOVERIES

"Discoveries in the natural sciences that enable mankind to dispose of increasingly powerful and varied forms of energy. To snare them and force them to serve us, once subdued. These are the most striking discoveries of our times.

"Less spectacular the discoveries in the realm of thought. Nevertheless, they are important. For there is progress to be made here, also, of which humanity has need. Through the ideas men have discovered and to which they have given their allegiance mankind has lifted itself from a primitive mentality to a state of civilization; because of the ideas conceived and circulated generation after generation civilization endures, progresses, and deepens." A. S., "*Paris Notes*"

"When in 1915 I outlined the new ethics of reverence for life I asked myself what its destiny would be. I thought that maybe after my death some candidate who wrote his doctoral thesis on philosophy would discover my papers and say: 'That's not so bad; it deserves some attention.'" A. S., "*Brussels Notes*"

"The good is reverence for life; it is extending ourselves to uphold life, to help it endure. Evil is to destroy life, to cause suffering. To help life reach full development, the good man is the friend of all living things." A. S., "*Paris Notes*"

"In the past, philosophy has been concerned with our spiritual relationship to the Absolute. The Absolute, for us, is something indefinable and remote. An enigma. But by practicing reverence for life we are in a spiritual relationship with the universe; we are in harmony with it."   A. S., *"Paris Notes"*

At the Günsbach organ

"As we acquire more knowledge, things do not become more comprehensible but more mysterious." A. S., "*Paris Notes*"

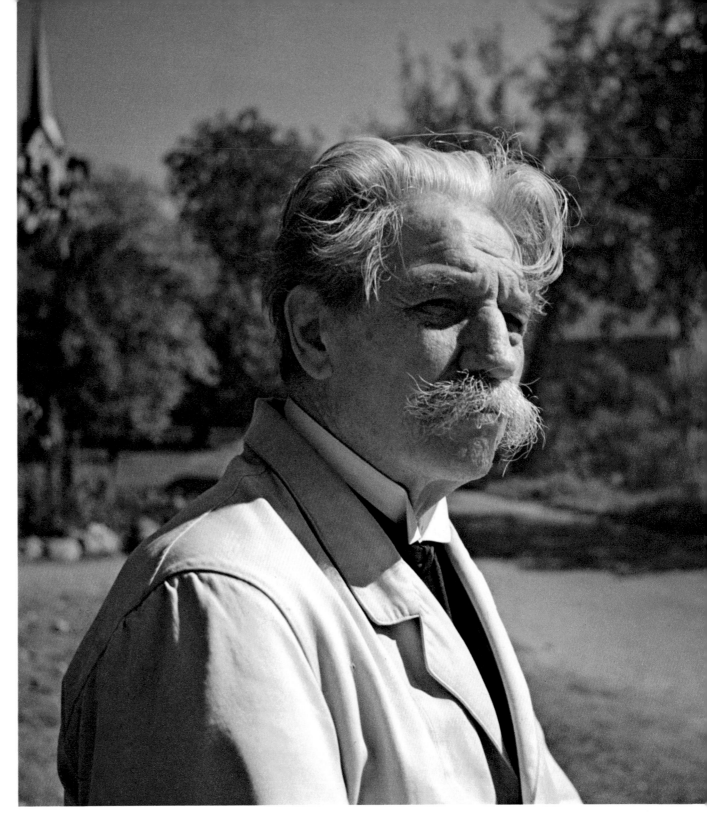

"Philosophic thought must be completely free."   A. S.

"Thought must be active. It must affect something."   A. S.

"When you portray me it should be not merely as the doctor who ministers to the sick. It is my philosophy that I consider my primary contribution to the world."   A. S.

"The beginning of all wisdom is to be filled with the mystery of existence and of life."   A. S., "*Paris Notes*"

On the Ogowe River, 1964

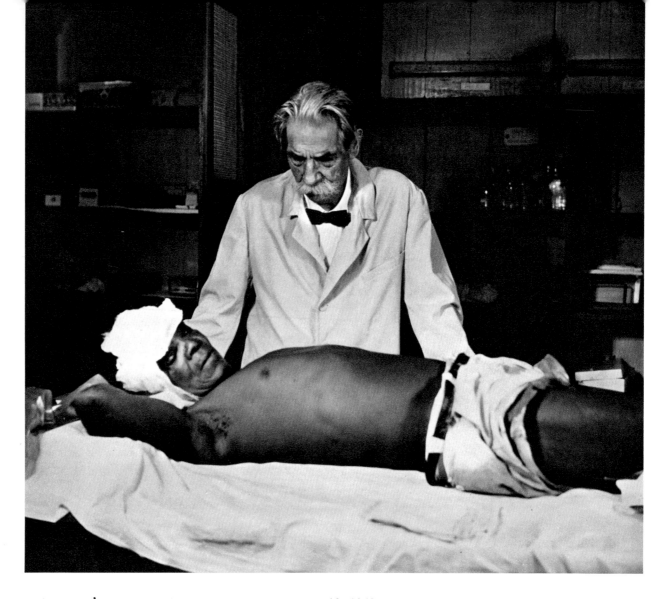

SCHWEITZER'S COMMENTS TO THE GABONESE ON APRIL 18, 1963, ON THE FIFTIETH ANNIVERSARY OF HIS ARRIVAL AT LAMBARENE.

I remember still the day when I completed my studies of medicine and when I talked with Monsieur Morel, a missionary at Lambarene. He said to me, "Come to us." And because he was Alsatian and so am I, I told myself, "I will go there." I did not think about it long, but said, "I have faith." My faith has not been mistaken. The mission permitted me to build a hospital, modest but good, and during long years I was able to serve this country through the mission hospital. And when the space for the mission became too small because I had more than 160 patients to house, I was forced to decide to hunt for a bigger place. It was the colonial government that offered the ancient territory of the king of the Galois to me. . . .

   And now I feel compelled to tell you how many times I have asked myself this question:
   —What would you have done if you hadn't been here?
   —What would you have done if you hadn't come?
   And always the result of my reflections is that good fortune brought me here to Lambarene, because at Lambarene I found what I was looking for: affection, confidence, and generosity. I have lived with you people of the Gabon during two wars. You had hardly any medicine, and I was permitted to do some useful work. Many friendships have been nourished between me and the people of the Gabon during and since the wars. And I am still here among you. I know this is a great honor, and it is of great benefit to me to stay here where I have established my work and where I am still useful in some ways. I confess to you: I feel at home here with you.

   And I do not know whether, if I had been elsewhere, all this sympathy would have been created among those who lived there and I who came. But the fact is that sympathy has been created between us, and that I will belong to you until my last breath. Thank you for all the sympathy that you have tendered me.

"Like all human beings, I am a person who is full of contradictions." A. S.

Schweitzer wears a white helmet by day against the ruthless sun, and an old brown felt hat after sundown. The mother of one of his friends told him before he went to Africa for the first time that in the tropics it was necessary to wear a hat after dark as well as by day. She made him promise always to wear one. The woman has long since died, but he kept his promise and still wears the same hat, though it is more than fifty years old, worn and full of holes.

At Kanzenrain, a hill near Günsbach where Schweitzer used to sit as a boy, 1957.

"Ethics are complete, profound, and alive *only* when addressed to all living beings. Only then are we in spiritual connection with the world. Any philosophy not respecting this, not based on the indefinite totality of life, is bound to disappear. . . .

"We find ourselves in a new movement of thought. In a movement where, through science and through the searching of our hearts, everything has become mysterious. Science has led us from knowledge to knowledge but also from mystery to mystery. Mystery alone can lead us on to true spirituality, to accept and be filled with the mystery of life in our existence. . . .

"Profound love demands a deep conception and out of this develops reverence for the mystery of life. It brings us close to all beings. To the poorest and smallest, as well as all others. We reject the idea that man is 'master of other creatures,' 'lord' above all others. We bow to reality. We no longer say that there are senseless existences with which we can deal as we please. We recognize that all existence is a mystery, like our own existence. The poor fly which we would like to kill with our hand has come into existence like ourselves. It knows anxiety, it knows hope for happiness, it knows fear of not existing any more. Has any man so far been able to create a fly? That is why our neighbor is not only man: my neighbor is a creature like myself, subject to the same joys, the same fears, and the idea of reverence for life gives us something more profound and mightier than the idea of humanism. It includes *all living beings*." A. S.

Brussels, 1959

174

"Everyone has his Lambarene."

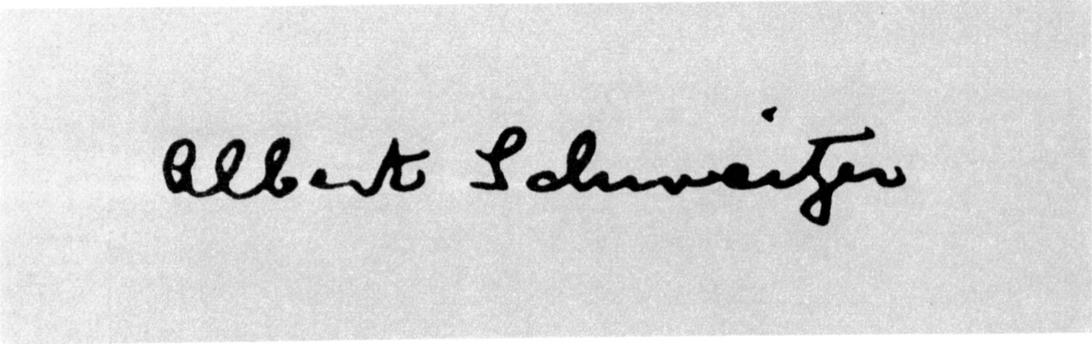

Albert Schweitzer